A Treasury of
Tennessee Tales

A Treasury of
Tennessee Tales

James Ewing

Rutledge Hill Press
Nashville, Tennessee

ISBN: 0-934395-04-7

Published in Nashville, Tennessee by Rutledge Hill Press, Inc., 513 Third Avenue South, Nashville, Tennessee 37210

Typography by ProtoType Graphics, Inc., Nashville, Tennessee
Printed and bound by Braun-Brumfield, Ann Arbor, Michigan

Library of Congress Cataloging in Publication Data

Ewing, James, 1917-
     A treasury of Tennessee tales.

     Includes index.
     1. Tennessee—History—Addresses, essays, lectures.
I. Title.
F436.5.E84   1985   976.8   85-18256
ISBN 0-934395-04-7

Printed in the United States of America
4   5   6   7   8   9   10   —   89

Introduction

A Treasury of Tennessee Tales is a collection of stories about interesting happenings that have occurred since the earliest days of the Volunteer State. These stories tell dramatic moments in the lives of such historical figures as Andrew Jackson, John Sevier, and William Blount. They relate the shenanigans of such desperadoes as Jesse James, John Murrell, and the Harpe brothers. There are tales about W. C. Handy, Casey Jones, and Fannie Battle, about Rock City, the Old Stone Fort, and the hanging of Murderous Mary, the circus elephant who killed a man in Kingsport in 1916.

The stories were selected and written with one objective in mind, to show that historical events can be interesting and thereby to encourage greater interest in Tennessee history among people of every age.

The genesis of this book goes back to 1968, when I was asked to write a series of articles to appear in the *Tennessee Conservationist*, to be called "Tennessee Tales." These articles, which appeared regularly over the next four years, provided a nucleus for this book, although the original tales have been updated and expanded and a number of new ones have been added.

I am indebted to many people for their help over years: Harry O'Donnell, information director for the Tennessee

Department of Conservation, who suggested the series back in the '60s; Mrs. Mary Glenn Hearne of the Nashville Room of the Public Library for her assistance in researching historical documents for use in the original columns and, more recently, for additional material to be used in the book; Senior U.S. District Judge Charles Neese for his suggestion of *A Treasury of Tennessee Tales* as the title for this book and for the information for the tale about moonshining; the late Nathaniel Jones for suggesting the book; my wife Alice for indexing and proofreading; and the people of Rutledge Hill Press, Larry Stone and Ron Pitkin, for their assistance.

James Ewing
Franklin, Tennessee

Table of Contents

PART ONE:
Colorful Characters

Murderous Mary swinging from a railroad derrick. Some questioned the authenticity of the picture.

Photo courtesy of the Tennessee Conservationist

1

Murderous Mary, the Elephant That Was Hanged

This has to be one of the weirdest happenings in Tennessee history. It's about an elephant that was hanged for the murder of her handler.

Some have questioned whether it ever occurred. The answer—confirmed by eyewitnesses and newspaper accounts of the time—is that it really did take place, although minor details of what caused the hanging and how many people saw it vary widely. Some parts of the story, as often happens, have improved with the telling.

For instance, some accounts incorrectly say that Mary killed a little girl; and estimates of the number who turned out to see "justice" done vary from two hundred to five thousand!

Here's the story, as pieced together from a number of accounts from witnesses and newspapers.

On September 12, 1916, the Sparks Brothers Circus was in Kingsport for a performance. Big Mary, billed as "The largest living land animal on earth—three inches taller than Jumbo and weighing over five tons" made a lunge for a lemonade stand. Her temporary trainer, Walter Eldridge, whacked her with a club. According to one account, the club struck her on an abscessed tooth.

Mary became furious, lifted Eldridge with her trunk, and dashed him to the ground. Accounts differ as to whether she also trampled him, but there was no questioning the fact that he died almost instantly.

The next day Mary was hanged on a railroad derrick at Erwin.

Some stories say that Mary was tried in a Tennessee court and sentenced to hang. That probably did not happen; for, then as now, the wheels of justice did not turn so swiftly. Witnesses recall a loud clamor among the people of the Kingsport area that Mary should be executed and the circus management appeared to agree with them. Reportedly the owner of the circus was nearby when Mary grabbed her trainer and felt that he had had a close call.

In any case, the only objectors appeared to be some of the circus women who had worked with the giant pachyderm and had known her as a gentle beast.

Why wasn't Mary disposed of in Kingsport? Witnesses said there wasn't a gun big enough in that part of the country to kill her. According to one account she was shot with a small bore pistol, and the bullets literally bounced off her tough hide.

Mary was taken to Erwin, where the Clinchfield Railroad was headquartered and where a derrick large enough to handle her could be found. On the first attempt, the chain which the handlers placed around her neck broke. That little mishap created pandemonium among those who had gathered to witness the hanging; they feared that Mary's next move might be to come after them.

The handlers then attached a stronger chain to her neck, and a short while later a local physician pronounced her dead. P. H. Flanary, a witness, later related, "We buried him [sic] with a steam shovel. I dug the grave after we hung [sic] the elephant . . . and also covered him [sic] with a steam shovel."

The hanging took place between four and five o'clock in the afternoon. It was a cloudy day, and local photographers had difficulty getting a good picture.

According to D. W. Love (Lieutenant Colonel, United States

Army—Retired) of Johnson City, the picture that appeared in the *Tennessee Conservationist* of June 1970 was said to have been taken by T. K. Broyles, brother-in-law of Colonel Love, who was employed by the Clinchfield Railroad at the time.

A somewhat similar drawing of Mary appeared in Robert Ripley's *Believe It or Not* of August 29, 1938. The inscription read: "Hanged for Murder: Mary, an elephant who killed 3 persons, was hanged from a railroad derrick! (No gun available that could penetrate her tough hide) Sparks Circus, Erwin, Tennessee, September 13, 1916."

Stories about the hanging also appeared in such popular magazines as *Argosy* and *Popular Mechanics*. An *Argosy* editor, when sent a photo of Mary hanging from the derrick, rejected it with the contention it was a "phony."

Another aspect of the story that seems to vary with which "witness" is telling it concerns Mary's behavior prior to the Kingsport killing. A circus public relations person said she had led an exemplary life and had never been known to harm anyone.

The Robert Ripley account, as quoted above, said she killed three persons. Others said her victims had numbered "six or seven."

An item titled *Wild Tigers and Tame Fleas* by Bill Ballantine (Rinehart & Company, 1958) provided this information on the general subject:

"In the old days, circuses simply hushed up a killing by an elephant (after all, wasn't a roughneck just an expendable nobody?), then changed the murderer's name and palmed the animal off on another show. Thus Queen, who choked her keeper to death with her trunk, a la boa constrictor, became Empress, a change which didn't deter her from killing five more persons on one bloody rampage. Under a third name, 'Mary,' she trampled a child during a street parade. Mary, to some accounts, was given a particular send-off. She was hanged from a railroad derrick."

2

Casey Jones, American Folk Hero

Jackson, Tennessee, was the hometown of John Luther Jones, better known as Casey Jones. Jones, who won immortality as one of America's truly great folk heroes, died in a railroad crash in which he was the only person who perished.

The crash occurred during the early morning of April 30, 1900, at Vaughan, Mississippi, when the *Cannonball Express* Jones was piloting hit the rear of a freight train.

Casey, thirty-six years old, had been with the Illinois Central for fifteen years, the last ten as an engineer. Jones earned the nickname "Casey" when he told fellow workers in Jackson that he had spent part of his boyhood in Cayce, Kentucky. Casey was easier to say—and spell—than Cayce or John Luther, and the nickname stuck.

Unlike many legendary heroes, Casey Jones was a real, living hero type, tall and handsome—six feet, four inches— with blue-gray eyes. Criticized by some as too reckless, he chalked up a number of infractions as a freight engineer. But after his promotion to passenger trains, three years prior to the crash, he kept a clean record.

At the time of the accident, trains were the fastest way to move the mails; and speed was at a premium. The Illinois Central had just set up its fastest schedule ever for the one hundred eighty-eight miles between Memphis and Canton,

Mississippi, just fourteen miles south of Vaughan, scene of the wreck.

Boys growing up during that time dreamed of working as an engineer on a big steam locomotive. They saw a five-year apprenticeship as a fireman, such as Jones served, as a small price to pay.

Many engineers developed distinctive styles that identified them to their admirers, young and old. Casey was no exception. He kept his big engine "super shiny," and he had his own "whippoorwill" whistle that had its own recognizable sound.

People knew that if they stood on the right side of the train engine and waved, they could get a "toot" or a wave from the engineer. On the engine's left side they could expect a wave from the fireman—if he wasn't too busy shoveling coal.

On the night of Casey's final run, his fireman, Sim Webb of Memphis, had his hands full shoveling coal. Casey had finished his south-north run to Memphis, and normally he would have gone home. But the engineer who was due to make the north-south run was ill, and Casey volunteered to make it for him.

When he left the Poplar Street Depot in Memphis, he was ninety-five minutes behind schedule. Casey vowed to make up the lost time by the time he reached Canton. During the one-hundred-two-mile run to Grenada, he made up fifty-five minutes, and he picked up another thirty minutes on the twenty-three miles to Winona. He then slowed to a speed that would have put him on schedule by the time he reached Vaughan.

In preparation for Casey's passage through Vaughan, the dispatchers had attempted to sidetrack two freight trains, one northbound and the other southbound.

The trains had more cars than the sidetrack could handle; so a "saw" was attempted. The idea was to move the end that was closest to the approaching locomotive, off the main track onto the sidetrack and to let the back end of the train on the south end stick onto the main line. The approaching

train would be stopped once it passed the north switch, and
the train on the siding could be pulled (or "sawed") forward
to let Casey and the *Cannonball Express* proceed south.

But several things went wrong. The standard procedure
was to explode torpedoes three thousand feet north of the station to stop the approaching train; the flagman was also to
proceed another five hundred feet up the line to swing a red
lantern and warn the oncoming train.

Jones and his fireman presumably neither saw the lantern
nor heard the exploding torpedoes. To make matters worse,
the train on the north end never cleared the main tracks due
to a broken air hose that locked the brakes and prevented it
from moving any farther.

When he rounded the curve at seventy-five miles per hour,
Casey applied his brakes, slowing the train to thirty-five
miles per hour by the time it collided with the caboose of the
southbound freight. Casey told his fireman to jump, which
he did, saving his life; and by the time the trains collided, the
impact was so reduced that no passenger received more than
minor injuries.

Thus Casey Jones was the only casualty, and he maintained
to the end his perfect record of never having lost a passenger.

One of Casey's admirers was a black engine wiper in the
Canton shops. He made up a little song about the "brave engineer," and one of those who heard it was an engineer named
William Leighton. Leighton's brothers, Bert and Frank, had
an Orpheum circuit vaudeville act. When they began singing
the song, it became an instant hit.

Carl Sandburg, the poet, called the song "Casey Jones, the
Brave Engineer," the "greatest ballad ever written." Certainly
it spawned a great number of other songs about engineers
and train wrecks (and they played a major part in the early
development of country music).

Over the years certain verses were added to the Casey Jones
song that were in poor taste and, moreover, were totally un-
true. Casey Jones, according to his closest friends, lived a

John Luther (Casey) Jones. A "real, living hero type."

clean life, was devoted to his wife, never caused talk about any kind of escapade, and never drank.

Tennesseans are fortunate that they can learn more about this popular hero of the great steam locomotive era by visiting the Casey Jones Museum at Jackson.

Among many items of interest at the museum is a replica of Casey's famous "whippoorwill" whistle made by his son, Charlie, a longtime expert mechanic on the Illinois Central line.

Note: The author of *A Treasury of Tennessee Tales* grew up at Vaughan where a first cousin, Mrs. T. H. Norman, Sr., now in her mid-nineties, is the only person still living who heard the wreck on that fateful morning in 1900. She visited the scene a short time afterward.

3

Fannie Battle, Nashville's Mother Teresa

Fannie Battle is remembered in Nashville as a kindly lady who spent the better part of her life helping needy and unfortunate children. Few know that she was a zealous supporter of the Confederate cause during the Civil War and spent time in a Federal prison for her spying activities.

During the Federal occupation of Nashville in 1862, Miss Battle, who was twenty years old at the time, joined other young women in dating Yankee soldiers, obtaining information from them, and passing it along to the Confederate command.

Living dangerously seemed to come naturally to the entire Battle family. Two brothers, William Searcy (actually a half-brother) and Joel, Jr., were killed at the Battle of Shiloh; and their father, Colonel Joel Battle, Sr., was captured at Shiloh because he refused to leave the battlefield until his sons had been found and identified.

Another brother, Captain Frank Battle, decided, while on leave to visit his family near Nashville, to go into Federally occupied Nashville with his sweetheart and see what the Yankees were doing.

Knowing he probably would be hanged if discovered, young Battle was careful to disguise himself as a girl. He was of a slim build and managed to wear his mother's and sisters' clothing. He also was careful to speak in a high-pitched voice.

Upon reaching the Federal picket line, he and his girlfriend were told that passes were no longer being honored, even for women. The girl took care of this problem by giving a bottle of wine to an officer of the guard.

Once Captain Battle and his girlfriend were behind Federal lines, things went well until a Union Army wagoner happened to back into their buggy. Captain Battle forgot his disguise momentarily and blasted the man with some strong language. Surprisingly, the Union man did not notice the change in language by the captain—perhaps he had already learned that some Southern belles possessed vocabularies more robust than the moonlight-and-roses tradition suggests.

Fannie Battle, however, was not so successful in deceiving the Federals. She was arrested as a spy and was sent to the Tennessee State Penitentiary, then located at Church Street and what is now 15th Avenue, North. She was later transferred to a prison at Washington, D.C., where she apparently stayed until the end of the war.

Fannie Battle's wartime experiences were but a prelude, however, to the life she would live. In 1870 Miss Battle, who had received her education at the Nashville Female Academy (predecessor of Ward's Seminary, Ward-Belmont, and eventually Belmont College), began teaching in the city's public schools.

When Nashville was ravaged by floods in December 1881, she led the effort for a relief society to aid the flood victims. Meeting with Mayor Thomas Kercheval and other leading citizens, Miss Battle persuaded them to form the Nashville Relief Society, which dispensed food, clothing, and coal to the destitute at the Capitol steps.

Fannie Battle used the flood relief effort as a wedge to convince the people of Nashville that a permanent, organized effort was needed to help the poor and victims of disasters. The resulting organization was named United Charities, and its headquarters was established in a residence on Market Street (Second Avenue).

In 1886, after pursuing her teaching career and doing charity work, too, she decided to give up teaching and to become secretary of United Charities. While schoolteachers of that era were woefully underpaid, her job with the charity organization required a substantial cut in pay. She would not have undertaken this task without her unselfish dedication to unfortunate people.

Later she wrote, "When I saw that the Society might become so discouraged it would cease its efforts, I knew there was only one thing I could do, and that was to give up my schoolteaching and throw my life, all of it, into the work."

A great-niece, Anne Elizabeth Battle, has confirmed that Miss Battle was motivated by a tragedy in her life—the death of the man she was to marry, in a railway accident on their wedding day. She resolved that henceforth she would give her life to "good works" and she held to that goal until the day of her death.

One day during the year 1891, Fannie Battle was driving a horse-drawn buggy along a street in North Nashville when she spied a crowd gathered on the side of the street. Good Samaritan that she was, she got out of her buggy to see what had happened.

Lying on the ground was an obviously undernourished boy crying from pain. She was told he had been struck by a wagon. Picking up the four-year-old, she took him to a hospital and set out to find his parents.

She discovered that the boy's father had deserted the mother and six children and that the mother was forced to work in a cotton factory, leaving the children to shift for themselves. Her investigation in the North Nashville area showed that several other families faced similar circumstances.

Thus began a new chapter in Fannie Battle's life. She rented a room in a house near the cotton mill—from her own limited means—and thus began Nashville's first day home.

Next she sought—and obtained—assistance from influential citizens to help find larger quarters and from physicians to donate their services for the unfortunate children. She also started a kindergarten.

In 1891, she also established the Addison Avenue (now 17th Avenue, North) Day Home, pioneering a kind of day care that was similar to those at London's Toynbee Hall (1884) and Jane Addams' Hull House in Chicago (1889).

In 1900 Miss Battle began a campaign for a "fresh air" camp to be open during summers for poor mothers and their children. This led to establishment of an 80-acre camp near Craggie Hope, about forty miles west of Nashville near Kingston Springs.

By 1916, hard times had befallen Miss Fannie's Day Home. With seventy children being served each day, the treasury had less than a dollar in it.

On December 14, a group of concerned ladies met at the home of Miss Frances Pilcher. Mrs. Eleanor Wills Rutland, the president, had a suggestion. An acquaintance had mentioned that in a church in her home town of St. Louis, Missouri, choirs sang carols on Christmas Eve at the home of every church member who burned a candle in a window, and donations were made for charitable purposes. The plan was worth trying.

Choirs from a number of churches and institutions, including the Fisk Jubilee Singers, responded to the call to "sing for Fannie Battle." Despite a heavy snowfall on December 19, the choirs covered downtown and many residential areas, collecting an "unbelievable" 787 dollars.

As Sara Sprott Morrow wrote in *The Legacy of Fannie Battle*, the singers "lighted a candle flame that has never dimmed as the seasons and generations pass." The phrase "a candle in every window, a carol at every door," originated by twelve-year-old Ernest Fisher who lived on Eastland Avenue in 1917, is still part of the tradition that continues to this day.

Newcomers to Nashville who are surprised to see singing groups—usually eight or ten young people, some very young, and one or more adults—at their doors singing carols at Christmastime, can now see what lies behind this old custom that began some seventy years ago.

Today the Fannie Battle Day Home, located at 911 Shelby Avenue, serves seventy-two children. It is a splendid testimony indeed to a woman who has been dead for more than fifty years.

Miss Battle died September 24, 1924, following a fall at Union Station. The *Nashville Banner* reported that she had gone to the station to accompany a group of children to the John W. Thomas Fresh Air Camp at Craggie Hope. The newspaper reported that Miss Battle's solicitude for a young girl who had been quite ill and "was frail" caused her to turn back at the gate leading to the train to urge the girl to follow her doctor's instructions "in order to regain her health." While returning to join the other children at the train gates, she stumbled over a suitcase, fell, and broke her hip.

Fannie Battle has been called "Nashville's most beloved woman" for good reason. To this day the Fannie Battle Social Workers operate the day home from funds obtained through the caroling program and contributions from parents capable of paying. There was help for a while from the old Community Chest, but the organization has chosen to operate without help from charitable agencies other than the federal school lunch program.

Note: In 1980 the Fannie Battle Social Workers published a book titled *The Legacy of Fannie Battle* written by Sara Sprott Morrow, former drama critic for the *Nashville Banner*. Celebrating the one hundredth anniversary of the founding of her noble cause and the two hundredth anniversary of Nashville, the book is also the story of organized charity in the city, 1881-1980.

4
The All-Night Ride of George Sloan

By the time Tennessee's James K. Polk was elected the eleventh president of the United States in 1844, the news was delivered in various ways. Whichever means could move the news the fastest was the method employed.

At this time the telegraph was in use, and the people of Nashville learned the good news about Polk's election very quickly. However, Polk was at his home forty miles to the south in Columbia, and the quickest way to inform him was to send someone on horseback.

That someone was a friend of Polk's, George Sloan. Upon learning of his election, Sloan mounted one of his best horses and rode all night to tell Polk of his victory. He had breakfast with Polk and then returned home to Nashville.

The news was particularly cheering to Polk, for he had learned that he failed to carry Tennessee; and he had assumed he had lost nationally, too. As it developed, he won by a sizable margin over Whig Henry Clay, receiving 170 electoral votes to Clay's 105. The popular vote was closer— 1,338,464 to Clay's 1,300,097.

Polk's parents, Samuel and Jane Knox Polk, had moved from North Carolina to the Columbia area in 1806. The oldest of ten children, James was "puny" and unable to join his heftier younger brothers at hard field chores. He spent much of his spare time at home in reading and study; and when he graduated from the University of North Carolina in 1818, he was at the top of his class.

He studied law with Felix Grundy, later to become a United States senator, who introduced him to Andrew Jackson. After winning and serving one term in the state House of Representatives, Polk ran for the United States House in 1825, winning the first of seven consecutive terms. Ten years later, with Jackson as president, Polk was elected speaker of the House. Later he was to become the only speaker ever to be elected president.

Meanwhile, in 1839, at the urging of his Democratic friend Andrew Jackson, Polk sought and won election as governor of Tennessee. After losing re-election bids in 1841 and 1843, he decided to challenge Martin Van Buren for the Democratic presidential nomination.

Because of his opposition to the annexation of Texas, Van Buren lost support among southern and western party members and failed to win the two-thirds vote needed for nomination. Polk was offered as a compromise candidate and he became the first "dark horse" to win a presidential nomination.

During his four years as president, Polk did something no other president since Washington had done: he fulfilled all his campaign promises. Those promises had been: to annex Texas; to acquire California; to settle the dispute with England over Oregon and maintain American rights there; to lower the tariff so it would be just to farmers and manufacturers alike thereby putting an end to the division between the agricultural South and the industrial North; and to put an end to financial chaos and bank controversy by creating a sub treasury, or Constitutional Treasury.

Polk's wife, Sarah Childress Polk, daughter of a wealthy Murfreesboro merchant, had a profound influence on his life. At no time was it more evident than during their White House years when, due to her strict religious views, card-playing, dancing, and alcoholic beverages were banned.

On June 15, 1849, just three months after he had left the

White House, Polk died in Nashville, the apparent victim of a cholera attack.

It is only within fairly recent times that historians have appreciated the significance of Polk's tenure. It was under him that America experienced its greatest territorial growth. In addition to the promised annexation of Texas, an area comprising nine Western states was placed under the American flag.

Like Washington, Polk was Commander-in-Chief of the military in fact as well as in name. Over the protests of some of his generals, he directed the Mexican War to its successful conclusion.

And now a final word about George Sloan, the Nashvillian who gave Polk the news of his presidential victory. Sloan was the first member of a family that was to become one of the city's most prominent.

In 1903 George Sloan's grandson Paul Lowe Sloan joined John E. Cain and Patrick M. Cain to open Cain-Sloan Company, a department store that still thrives in Nashville. Paul and Ann Joy Sloan's son, John E. Sloan, was a long-time president of the store, which in recent years has been sold to Allied Stores, a national chain.

John E. Sloan, and his sons, appear to have inherited George Sloan's love of horses. John Sloan was an organizer of the Hillsboro Hounds and a co-founder of the internationally famous Iroquois Steeplechase. George and Paul Sloan, sons of John E. Sloan, became avid steeplechase riders; and in 1970 George won the United States Amateur championship, while Paul was runner-up.

In 1977-78 George Sloan was the first American to win the prestigious Amateur Championship in England. Since steeplechasing originated in England, one writer commented that Sloan's winning it was comparable to a group of Englishmen organizing a baseball team and coming to the United States and defeating the Dodgers.

The *London Times* commented: "Mr. Sloan sits well on his horses, presents them correctly at their fences, and lacks nothing in courage . . . He has even captured the attention of the Queen Mother, who is a steeplechasing enthusiast."

After all, though, what would you expect from a man whose great-great-grandfather and namesake rode a horse from Nashville to Columbia as if it were just an evening's outing?

5

W. C. Handy, the Father of the Blues

Here's a trivia question for music lovers, particularly those who lean to jazz and blues: What was W. C. Handy's first musical instrument?

If you say a horn, a violin or a piano, you're wrong. It was a guitar and had he been able to keep it he might have become a B. B. King or a Chet Atkins.

When William Christopher Handy was eight years old and living in Florence, Alabama, he managed to scrape together enough money to buy a guitar. But his father, a minister who considered professional musicians sinners, made him return the instrument and trade it for a dictionary.

At the age of thirteen, Handy bought a cornet, paying $1.75 for it. Presumably by then his father had become more tolerant. After he mastered the cornet, Handy met a musician from Memphis who taught him to play the violin. Later he learned to play the piano and capitalized on his excellent tenor voice to teach voice and to sing with his own band.

Handy studied voice and music at Alabama's Agricultural and Mechanical College in Huntsville. He went to Memphis at thirty years of age as a band director. From that position he moved into the professional ranks as a dance band leader. During those early years Handy played songs with a traditional beat, but he noticed that people of both races seemed attracted to a kind of music with sharps and flats that gave it a special sound.

Handy perfected the technique, and the blues was born. He quickly became Memphis' most popular band leader. Meanwhile, he set out to write songs that would use the blues sound. His first was the campaign song for a gentleman running for mayor, E. H. Crump. Crump later became one of the nation's most powerful mayors, with the informal title "Boss Crump." Boss Crump won that first election by a narrow margin, and one might ask what would have happened to his career if Handy had worked for one of his rivals instead.

After Crump took office, he gave Handy permission to rename the song he had written "Memphis Blues." This was the first of many songs that would combine to make him world famous.

Handy was tricked by a white music shop operator who convinced him that "Memphis Blues" was not selling very well; so Handy sold it to him for one hundred dollars. Fortunately, Handy later regained ownership of the song, and it brought him thousands of dollars in royalties.

Interestingly, Handy's most famous song, "St. Louis Blues," had a slow start. He tried for two years without success to sell it to major publishers, and they all rejected it. Then he persuaded a girl to sing it for Victor records. The record became an instant hit, and Handy became a wealthy man from its royalties.

Although Handy lived less than fifteen of his eighty-five years in Memphis, that Tennessee city always has claimed him as its own, and still does. It has honored him in many ways. The square at Beale and Third was named Handy's Park, and a statue of Handy and his famous horn was erected there. Later, a scholarship memorial fund was established in his name.

Florence, Alabama, his boyhood home, also honored him, restoring his home in the Handy Heights neighborhood and enshrining his trumpet and piano.

Although Handy was obviously more liberal-minded than his father and grandfather, both of whom were preachers, he was deeply religious throughout his life. The blindness he suffered early in his career seemed to deepen his faith, and certainly his blindness did not cramp his style as a band leader or as a songwriter.

He composed at least five spiritual songs for every blues number. His favorite spiritual, "They That Sow in Tears Shall Reap in Joy," premiered in 1955 at the Overton Park Shell in Memphis and was sung by the Pendleton Presbyterian Choir.

Handy, who was born November 16, 1873, died March 28, 1958. He became one of Memphis' most widely known citizens; and the late Paul Coppock, Memphis historian and newspaperman, wrote that "It is doubtful if anyone has done more to make Memphis famous."

6

When "Injun Sam" Swung a Mean Whip

Some say it is a legend and some say it really happened. But if it did happen, it would have been a strange sight that greeted General Andrew Jackson and his trusted aide, Captain John Reid, as they arrived on horseback at the small village of Maryville on a cold morning in March, 1813. The crowd that had originally come to hear the general speak was now preoccupied with the preliminaries to one of the frontier's most cruel forms of amusement—a whip race.

The three-man welcoming committee had for the moment forgotten its purpose. As the judges of the contest, its members were busy laying out the quarter-mile-long course down which the two combatants would soon be running as hard as their swift legs would carry them.

The principals in the race were Mike Hooten, the town bully, a burly fellow who wore a red turkey feather in his hat signifying that he had also been cock of the walk on his keelboat on a voyage down the Mississippi to New Orleans and a tall, cleancut young lad known to the townsfolk as "Injun Sam."

Spoiling for a fight, the bully, a hairy ape of a fellow with a huge chest, bulldog neck, and big, brawny arms and fists, had picked on a callow young fellow who made the mistake of standing too close to him when the bully was challenging one and all to a fight.

Hooten was in the act of making the hapless victim down a mouthful of dirt when "Injun Sam" laid a hand on his shoulder and ordered him to stop it.

Enraged, Hooten turned on Sam with the fury of a tornado. "Tell ye what I'm agonna do," he said. "I'm goin' to make you eat some of the same dirt as Alec did."

"I heard you make your brags, Hooten," said Sam.

"So?"

"You bragged you could outrun any man here, I dare you to a whip race."

Under the rules of this frontier sport, a coin was tossed to determine which of the two would be the first to wield the five-foot cowhide whip. They would line up five paces (fifteen feet) apart and, at the drop of a handkerchief by one of the judges, begin their mad dash down the quarter-mile course. The objective of the man with the whip was to lay as many lashes on his foe as possible. The latter, of course, attempted all the while to stay ahead of those punishing rawhide tassels.

Sam won the toss of the coin but, to the surprise of the crowd, told Hooten he could be the first to wield the whip. This was a distinct advantage, since one good blow of the whip might be enough to slow the man down when it became his turn.

At the drop of the handkerchief, the two men sped down the course, Hooten swinging the whip several times but falling just inches short of reaching the fleeing Sam.

In a blind rage, Hooten ignored the rules of the contest and planted a vicious blow of the whip on Sam's back after they passed the finish mark. Practicing self-control, Sam waited for the five-minute "blowing period" before they began the race back up the village street.

Hooten soon discovered that his younger adversary had been playing a game with him. He was a much faster runner than he had appeared, and the bully began to feel the stings of the whiplash with regularity.

Halfway down the course, Hooten violated the rules again.

He stopped suddenly in his tracks and attacked his young pursuer. Clawing and kicking, he sought to disable his adversary. Just when it began to appear that Sam was going to have an eye gouged out, he managed to pull out of Hooten's grasp and to lay on him what would, in modern-day terminology, be called a shoestring tackle.

Hooten fell hard to the ground, his breath knocked out of him. The contest was over.

After his address to the crowd, General Jackson asked to meet the young "Injun Sam." It marked the beginning of a warm friendship with the man who was later to be called "Governor" in Tennessee and Texas—Sam Houston.

7

The Fountain of Youth on the Mississippi

While most of us are familiar with the story of Ponce de León and his search in Florida for a "Fountain of Youth," another story concerns an equally famous Spaniard, Hernando de Soto, who made a search through Tennessee for such a mystic fountain. De Soto's quest led him to the Mississippi River and the Indian home of the Great Chief Chisca, who lived in seclusion atop an ancient mound.

The Spanish general and his army of several hundred had landed in Tampa Bay on the coast of Florida in May, 1539. They spent two years making their way through Florida and the wilds of what is now Tennessee, losing scores of men to the arrows of savage Indians, to pestilence and disease. De Soto, according to the story, was about to give up the search and turn back when an Indian brave communicated the news that just a little farther west lay the mighty "Father of Waters," a fountain of eternal youth and a great Indian chief who remained young and strong because he drank from the fountain.

Great Chief Chisca had lived in seclusion in his mound home for many years. His lodge was surrounded by a strong wall of logs and could be reached only by climbing two ladders placed one above the other against the steep side of the mound. A group of chosen warriors guarded him night and day. Only his nearest of kin, his counselors, and the "mystery man" of the Chickasaw tribe were allowed to climb the ladders.

It was well-known that he had once been a strong young warrior, and the legend grew that he retained all his youthful abilities and appearance as he grew wiser through the years with age. Neighboring tribes heard the story and did not dare to attack the Chickasaw Bluff home of the Great Chisca. They felt that in discovering the mystery of youth he had attained supernatural powers.

When de Soto and his men reached the area that is now Memphis and looked for the first time on the waters of the mighty Mississippi, it only made the story of Chisca's greatness more believable. Entering the village inhabited by the Chickasaws, they had no difficulty in subduing them with their sticks that shot fire and the strange animals they rode, for the Indians had never laid eyes on guns or horses.

Even so, some four thousand warriors surrounded their chief at his mound home and de Soto found himself temporarily foiled. But he immediately set out to win over the chief. He finally accomplished this by sending gifts and by a veiled suggestion that he, too, possessed supernatural powers.

Finally, the great day came; and de Soto was permitted to scale the ladders and visit the Great Chief Chisca inside the royal lodge where only a handful of men, white or red, had ever been. Brushing eagerly past the deerhide door of the chief, de Soto came to a full halt a few scant feet from the object of his interest. There he beheld, not a young, virile warrior, but a wizened little man, skinny and wrinkled with a high, cackling voice and glazed eyes that made it difficult for him to see his visitor.

Stammering a few brief words, de Soto quickly made his exit, still in a state of shock over the little mummy-like creature he had beheld. Gathering the remnants of his army, he built rafts and crossed the Mississippi. He continued his quest for the elusive fountain for another year before continuing southward toward the Gulf of Mexico.

As it turned out, de Soto was very much in need of the

youth-renewing waters he sought so diligently. He died in 1542, before completing his trip down the Mississippi, just one year after his meeting with the Great Chief Chisca.

More than a hundred years passed before another white man viewed the Mississippi. This time it was a Frenchman, La Salle, who planted a banner on the old site of Chisca and built a cabin and fort.

PART TWO:
Strange Bedfellows

Brothers Bob (Left) and Alf Taylor fiddlin' for votes as they vied
in 1886 for the office of governor of Tennessee.
Cartoon from Frank Leslie's Illustrated Newspaper, Oct. 2, 1886

8

The War of the Roses

Ask the average Tennessean who Bob and Alf Taylor were, and he'll probably tell you they were a couple of brothers—one a Republican and the other a Democrat—who campaigned against each other for governor in the late 1800's in the famed War of the Roses. Beyond that, most are inclined to become rather vague.

Which one was the Republican? Which one won? Where did that name "War of the Roses" come from? Was it a friendly rivalry, or did they hate each other?

Without getting too involved, we'll give you just a little background that will help explain the rivalry.

The Taylor household was divided, in a sense, when the boys were born. Their father, Nathaniel G. Taylor, a lawyer and Methodist preacher, served in the Congress as a Whig from the old First District in northeastern Tennessee. Like many other East Tennesseans, he was a strong supporter of the Union during the Civil War.

But his wife, Emmeline, was the sister of Landon Carter Hayes, a Confederate senator from Tennessee; and her sympathies were with the South. So, the boys had a lot to argue about while toiling on their father's farm in Happy Valley, Carter County.

Alfred A. Taylor was the older of the two and the one destined to become a Republican. He was born in 1848. Robert Love Taylor, Democrat, was born in 1850.

It was due to a political misfortune of Alf's that Bob first entered politics. Shortly after being admitted to the bar in 1878, Alf sought the Republican nomination for Congress; but the committee gave it to his rival, A. H. Pettibone.

Democratic leaders then prevailed on Bob Taylor to run for the office. With the help of many rank and file Republicans who thought Alf got a dirty deal, Bob was elected, even though the First District, then as now, was normally rock-ribbed Republican.

After a single term in Congress, Bob failed to win re-election; but he didn't give up politically. When Grover Cleveland ran for President in 1884, Bob Taylor stumped the state for him and won more friends. He served as a presidential elector and after Cleveland's election was appointed pension agent for Knoxville.

Meanwhile, Alf had not given up his ambitions for public office. When the Republicans met in Nashville in June 1886 to choose their gubernatorial nominee, Alf won on the first ballot.

Two months later, the Democrats met in Nashville (this was before the days of primary elections) and, on the fifteenth ballot, chose brother Bob Taylor.

The stage was set for a brother-against-brother "knock-down-drag-out" battle, and excitement began to build from one end of the state to the other.

Unlike many of their modern-day counterparts, the Taylors did not shy away from debates (after all, they didn't have to worry about TV shadow),and so their campaign managers worked out a schedule that would take them on a series of forty-one debates throughout the state.

The first was held on September 9 in Madisonville. Bob set the tone by declaring, "I have a very high regard for the Republican candidate—he is a perfect gentleman because he is my brother. I have already told him to come with me and I would furnish him with crowds and introduce him to society. We are two roses from the same garden."

Throughout the tour the brothers traveled together and even slept in the same bed (what's the one about politics and strange bedfellows?). On occasion, their remarks during the debates became biting, but there were never hard feelings between them.

Perhaps the closest the Taylors came to hard feelings was during a visit to Chattanooga when Bob played a practical joke on Alf.

When they arrived in Chattanooga they were met with a gala welcome prepared by a joint Republican and Democratic committee. Both were determined to make the best speeches possible from their hotel balcony. Alf had worked particularly hard on his, preparing a totally new manuscript for the occasion.

Then Alf was called out of the hotel to meet some friends. A short time later Bob began his speech, and Alf was shocked when he heard a familiar phrase. After listening for a moment, he exclaimed, "Great Scott! Listen! He is quoting the text of my speech, word for word. . . ."

And a beautiful speech it was as Bob intoned, "The illustrious dreamers and creators in the realm of music, the Mozarts, the Beethovens, the Handels and the Mendelssohns, have scaled the purple steeps of the heaven of sweet sounds, unbarred its opal gates and opened its holy of holies to the rapt ear of the world. In their wonderful creations of melody they have given a new interpretation and a sweeter tongue to nature and an audible voice to the music of the stars. Surely humanity can never forget God or our civilization sink to a lower plane while their works endure."

Alf rushed to his room, and his fears were confirmed. The manuscript was nowhere to be found. Bob had purloined it, and he didn't stop until he had read it in its entirety.

Like any good politician, Alf rose to the occasion and made his speech extemporaneously. It wasn't the one he had planned, though; and no doubt it was considerably less flowery than the one his brother had read.

The tour attracted nation-wide interest. Followers met them at train stations, with Bob's supporters wearing white roses and Alf's wearing red roses.

Despite Bob's remark about their both being "two roses from the same garden," the name "War of the Roses" was adopted from the famous fifteenth-century fight for the throne in England when the House of York opposed the House of Lancaster. The Democrats adopted the white rose of York and the Republicans the red rose of Lancaster.

The two candidates sought to entertain the crowds with music and repartee, rather than "confuse them with issues." Both played the fiddle; and, while Alf was better in this department, Bob made up for it with his sharp wit.

On one occasion, Bob remarked that, while both were born of the same mother and nursed at the same breast, Alf's milk soured on him and he became a Republican.

In his closing speech of the campaign, Bob told the audience, "I say to you now that after all these eventful struggles I still love my brother as of old, with an undying affection—but politically, my friends, I despise him."

A few days later, Bob was declared the winner, by a thirteen thousand-vote majority. Ten years later, he again heeded the urgings of his Democratic friends and was elected to another term. He also served Tennessee as a United States senator.

Meanwhile, Alf did not give up. He served three terms in Congress and in 1921 realized his ambition to become governor—at the ripe, young age of seventy-two!

9

Tennessee's David and Goliath

Tennessee had its own David and Goliath back in the early days before statehood.

John Sevier was about to undertake another campaign against the Cherokees, and he sent out a call for volunteers to assist him in an attack on their town of Etowah. Among the volunteers was young Hugh Lawson White, son of James White, founder of Knoxville. White, a scholar also schooled in the art of warfare, went along as an aide to Sevier.

Leading the Cherokees in their defense was their chief, King Fisher. In the thick of the fighting a bullet from one of Sevier's volunteers struck and instantly killed Chief King Fisher. The bullet came from the rifle of Hugh Lawson White.

In total disarray after the fall of their leader, the rest of the tribe abandoned Etowah and fled into the forest. Sevier followed his accustomed practice and ordered the town burned to the ground.

Unlike David of biblical times, White did not go on to become a great warrior. The death of the Indian chief and the destruction of the town were so revolting to him that he vowed never to fight again.

White nevertheless became one of Tennessee's great leaders, and later in life he earned the title "Hugh Lawson White the Just." As a young man he received private tutoring from two of the territory's outstanding scholars, the Reverend Samuel Carrick, a Presbyterian minister, and Archibald Roane, graduate of Liberty Hall Academy (forerunner of Washington and Lee University) and an attorney who later would serve as governor of Tennessee.

In 1793, White became a private secretary to Governor William Blount of the Tennessee Territory. The following year he went to Philadelphia to study mathematics for a year, after which he spent a year in Lancaster, Pennsylvania, studying law.

He began the practice of law in Knoxville in 1796. Five years later he was elected a superior judge, or judge of the state's highest court. He served for six years before resigning to enter politics and win a seat in the state senate.

He served until 1809, when he resigned to become a member of the newly organized State Supreme Court. He served on the court until 1814; but when the Bank of Tennessee was established in 1811, he was elected its president. Thus he served for three years in the dual position of a justice of the Supreme Court and president of the state bank.

White left the high court in 1814 to give full attention to the bank presidency, which he held until 1827. In 1821, while he was still bank president, White was appointed by President James Monroe as one of three commissioners of claims for the transfer of Florida from Spain to United States rule.

In 1825, now both a bank president and a United States claims commissioner, White was elected United States senator, succeeding a man he had come to know well, Andrew Jackson.

Two incidents, one in which he defied his old friend Jackson, served to show White's integrity. As his second term drew to a close in 1835, Jackson sought to name Martin Van Buren as his successor. Many Tennesseans, including White, considered Jackson's tactics as "high-handed," and consequently White accepted nomination by the General Assembly as a candidate for president. Although he knew he would not win, White had the satisfaction of carrying Tennessee by a majority of ten thousand, despite opposition from both Jackson and James K. Polk.

In 1839, while still a member of the United States Senate, White objected to an action by the Tennessee General Assembly in which it sought to instruct the senators in how to vote. To emphasize his feelings in the matter, White resigned. The following year he died.

10

The Hero Who Could Not Be Impeached

Few examples of loyalty by citizens of an entire state can match that shown by Tennesseans to the popular William Blount following his expulsion from the United States Senate in 1797.

Blount had served as the first governor of the Southwest Territory, also known as the Territory South of the River Ohio. After Tennessee achieved statehood in 1796, he, with William Cocke, was elected to serve in the United States Senate.

Blount, with a perfect record of service to his state and his country, became the first member to be expelled from the Senate. While historians have since agreed that Blount's expulsion was politically motivated, he took little comfort in the fact while he lived.

At the time Tennessee sought statehood—1796—John Adams and Thomas Jefferson were waging a fierce battle for the presidency. It was well known in the capital, Philadelphia, that both Blount and John Sevier, the two most powerful men in the new state, would favor Jefferson over Adams.

Tennessee became the sixteenth state in time to cast three votes for Jefferson in his losing battle with Adams. Adams no doubt got his chance for revenge sooner than he had dared hope. It came in the form of a letter that Blount supposedly had written to James Carey, his interpreter among the Indians in the Knoxville area.

At the time, Spain was at war with Great Britain, the latter being interested in acquiring Louisiana. Many Americans, including Adams and Blount, were sympathetic to Britain; but Adams had campaigned on a platform of neutrality in the conflict, which was the United States' official position.

But the letter purportedly written by Blount to Carey contained an outline of a plot to aid the British against Spain. The letter, dated April 21, 1797, was cautiously worded, asking Carey to "keep things in proper frame for action in case it should be attempted. You must take care in whatever you say . . . ," it continued, "not to let the plan be discovered . . . . If I attempt this plan, I shall expect to have you and all my Indian country and Indian friends with me, but you . . . are not to say anything . . . until you again hear from me. . . . When you have read this letter over three times, burn it."

Carey did not burn the letter. While drunk, he showed it to a Knoxvillian who worked for the Spanish minister to the United States. He, in turn, wrote an angry letter to President Adams; and Adams, in turn, expressed shock and dismay that the Tennessee senator would do such a thing.

According to some accounts, Adams, along with his top aides, Alexander Hamilton and Secretary of State Timothy Pickering, had conceived the plot to help Britain. Blount was to play a minor role in it. In any event, Adams saw the Carey letter as a way to even the score with Blount and damage the "Democratick" party in the bargain. Adams ordered that the letter be read to both houses of Congress, suggesting that the Senate expel Blount and the House begin plans for impeachment.

Blount was taking a walk when the letter was read to the Senate; but upon his return, the letter was read again for his benefit. Five days later the Senate voted to expel Blount by a vote of twenty-five to one. Blount was given no opportunity to defend himself and was released under bond. As plans for his impeachment were begun, a sadder but wiser Blount returned to his home in Knoxville, then the capital of the state.

William Blount could not have been more surprised at the

welcome he received. James White, founder of Knoxville, and a large group of Knoxvillians gave Blount a rousing welcome. They conducted him triumphantly to his mansion, which had served both as his home and office when he was governor of the Tennessee Territory.

As the time neared for Blount's trial, James Matthers, Sergeant-at-Arms for the United States Senate, was dispatched to Tennessee to arrest him. Upon his arrival, Matthers was greeted by Blount and other high officials as if he had come for a social visit; and they entertained him for several days at Blount Mansion.

Somewhat nonplussed at this attitude, Matthers finally got to the business for which he came. He appealed for a posse to escort Blount back to Philadelphia (after the United States marshal had refused to arrest him), but not a single man volunteered. Matthers headed back to Philadelphia empty-handed. He was soon joined by a group of citizens who assured him William Blount would never be returned to Philadelphia.

But Tennesseans were not through showing their affection for and confidence in their deposed senator. In 1798, when James White resigned as Senate speaker to become Indian Commissioner for the state of Tennessee, the voters of Knox County elected Blount to succeed him in the state Senate; and the members of that body lost no time in electing him speaker.

Meanwhile, impeachment proceedings finally began in the United States Senate, but they were of short duration. Blount's attorneys pointed out that, having been expelled, he was no longer a member of the Senate, and thus not subject to its deliberations. No trial was held, and the charges were dismissed. The Senate decision came on February 11, 1799. Blount died the following year of a fever, at the age of fifty-three. His name was still under a cloud, as far as the national scene was concerned.

Several years later, Blount's half brother, Willie Blount, who had served as his secretary and protégé, wrote an explanation of the entire mess for the benefit of William Blount's children. It was apparently a convincing account for both the Blount children and posterity, for today William Blount continues to rate high in the estimation of Tennesseans and others throughout the country who have studied his career.

All of which leads to the question, "Did William Blount really write that letter?"

The respected historian J. G. M. Ramsey wrote: "Whatever foundation there may have been for the impeachment of William Blount, and whatever truth there may have been in the charge preferred against him, there was no one in Tennessee who viewed his conduct as criminal, unpatriotic, or unfriendly to the true interests of the state or the West, and all refused to sanction the proceedings against him."

Some historians accept the letter as having been written by Blount. Certainly he had a motive, for he had extensive land holdings in the western part of the state and their value had dropped to the point that he was threatened with bankruptcy (he had transferred his property to his half brother Willie). British control of the Mississippi River would have enhanced the value of all western lands.

But even assuming he wrote the letter, his biggest mistake appeared to be a lack of discretion. Perhaps he should have heeded the advice of the poet who suggested to lovers, "say it with flowers, but never in writing."

11

Sevier vs. Jackson: Tennessee's Greatest Nonduel

Without a doubt, the two outstanding figures in Tennessee at the turn of the century of the 1800s were John Sevier and Andrew Jackson. Both were strong-willed, both were professional fighting men, and both were fiercely proud of their accomplishments and capabilities.

In 1801 Sevier had just completed three two-year terms as Tennessee's first governor and was prohibited by the Constitution from serving another term consecutively. Archibald Roane, a highly qualified lawyer, sought and won election as the young state's second governor.

A few months into Roane's term, a vacancy occurred in the military, that of major general of the state's militia. Sevier, age fifty-seven, veteran of many Indian battles and a former brigadier general in the militia, applied for the job.

So did thirty-five-year-old Andrew Jackson. While Jackson's military experience did not compare with that of Sevier's—the Battle of New Orleans was still fourteen years in the future—Jackson had a very strong point in his favor. He was Roane's former law partner.

The military post was filled through election by its commissioned officers, but the vote ended in a tie. Governor Roane broke the tie by casting a vote for his old friend Jackson. Sevier vowed he would oust Roane in the next gubernatorial election, and he did so by a handsome majority. The

Constitution provided that after being out of office for as little as two years, a former governor could then seek three more consecutive two-year terms; and John Sevier did just that.

But Governor Roane did not give in without a struggle. When he announced that he would seek a second term, his old pal Jackson was there to help him. And Jackson held a trump card in his hand. As Superior Judge for East Tennessee, he was privy to considerable information about land deals dating back to the 1770's.

Jackson charged that Sevier had acquired considerable land in a deal with a North Carolina official named James Glasgow and had paid off Glasgow with part of the land. Governor Roane used the "scandal" against Jackson in the campaign of 1803, but Sevier and his backers came back with the charge that Roane had pardoned a young man convicted of murder. Roane branded that accusation a lie. The election ended the contest, but the bitter feelings lingered.

Shortly after Sevier's inauguration, while Jackson was holding court in Knoxville, the two met on the public square. Sevier violently denounced Jackson, and Jackson replied in kind. The encounter that followed is described in James Phelan's *History of Tennessee* as follows:

> The two men had many points in common. Both had a gracious and winning suavity of speech and gentleness of manner when calm. Both were subject to frantic outbursts of fury. And both, when enraged, were like madmen. They stormed. They blustered. They swore loud and boisterous oaths. Their faces and lips grew white. Their eyes glistened like melted glass. And like wild beasts, the first impulse of each was to strike, to wound, to tear. But each had also a reserve of prudence that was rarely extinguished even in the most violent paroxysms.
>
> Jackson's anger flamed out at (a) reference to his wife, and he made desperate efforts to reach Sevier, but was restrained. Jackson, seeing his antagonist with a drawn cutlass, and having only a cane himself, prudently yielded to the remonstrances of the bystanders. The next day, he sent a challenge.

Sevier returned a mocking reply, accepting for any time and place "not within the State of Tennessee." Jackson insisted on the meeting taking place in the neighborhood of Knoxville, since the insult had been passed here. Sevier declined. "I have some respect," said he, "for the laws of the state over which I have the honor to preside, although you, a judge, appear to have none." Charges and countercharges were hurled back and forth, verbally and in writing. Jackson suggested several times and places for the duel, Sevier refused them all, not even opening Jackson's letters. Jackson went to Southwest Point, near Knoxville, at the time he had appointed in one of his letters to meet Sevier, but Sevier did not come. On the way back to Knoxville, Jackson and his party met Sevier riding with a group of friends.

Enraged, Jackson charged upon him with his cane. Sevier dismounted. Pistols were drawn. But Jackson had lost all stomach for the fight, and Sevier had never had any. Friends intervened. After some wrangling, an indifferent peace was patched up between them. . . . Sevier had seventeen children. Sevier's death at Jackson's hands meant also Jackson's death at the hands of Sevier's sons, who were proud, brave, and devoted to him. This undoubtedly had much to do with the hair-splitting niceties of the correspondence by which a meeting was successfully evaded.

Today statues of the two men stand in the national Capitol, nobly representing the Volunteer State as two of her greatest.

12

General Jackson at the Racetrack

Two incidents occurring at the Clover Bottom Racetrack on Stone's River between Donelson and the Hermitage show two sides of Andrew Jackson: as a fierce leader of men and the one time in his adult life when he was cast in the role of a squirming, protesting child.

The former occurred during one of the truly big race events attended by some twenty thousand people. As Jo Conn Guild, author of *Old Times in Tennessee*, tells it, betting had been heavy for this particular race—there was a large "pound" of slaves and horses that had been wagered on the outcome.

"I heard some loud talking," Guild, who was a lad at the time, wrote, "and, looking down the track saw, for the first time, Gen. Jackson, riding slowly on a gray horse, with long pistols held in each hand. As General Jackson led the van and approached the judges' stand, he was rapidly talking and gesticulating. As he came by me he said that he had irrefutable proof that this was to be a jockey race; that Grey Hound (one of the horses) was seen in the wheat field the night before; which disqualified him for the race, and that his rider was to receive five hundred dollars to throw the race; and 'by the Eternal God' he would shoot the first man who brought his horse upon the track; that the people's money should not be stolen from them in this manner. He talked incessantly while the fire sparkled from his eyes.

"I have seen bears and wolves put at bay, but he was certainly the most ferocious looking animal that I have ever seen. His appearance and manner struck terror into the hearts of 20,000 people."

Needless to say, the owners of Grey Hound did not push their case. The horse was withdrawn, and the bettors surged forward and reclaimed the property that had been put on the line.

This was the Andrew Jackson people in the early 1800s knew; the firebrand, the hothead, the impulsive, hard-living leader of men, the righter of wrongs, the man no one dared cross.

But he did get his comeuppance one day, and he took it like a schoolboy being disciplined for doing what he knew was wrong. This time, the scene was the same: the Clover Bottom Racetrack. Only the horses were different. Jackson, in his boyish enthusiasm for a Kentucky nag named Yellow Jacket, wanted to wager ten thousand dollars that Jacket could beat a filly named Maria.

General John Coffee, Jackson's most trusted friend, business associate, and a relative by marriage, tried to talk him out of making the bet. He was having little success with the impetuous soldier, farmer, statesman and horse lover. Suddenly, General Coffee did something no other man had ever attempted or even thought of attempting. He lifted Jackson bodily and carried him kicking, squirming, and protesting from the field of action—and continued to hold him in his powerful grasp until the race was over. It was later reported that, despite his apparent fearlessness, General Coffee breathed a sign of relief when his hunch proved correct and Yellow Jacket was beaten by Maria.

You can appreciate Coffee's feat better if you know a little more about the man. Physically, he was a giant, standing six feet, eight inches high. James Parton described him as a "man of the mighty arm and massive fist, and thundering voice, and face of bronze, and heart of oak; the backwoodsman's beau-ideal of a colonel of hunting-shirted dragoon."

JOHN COFFEE.

General John Coffee, a 6-foot, 8-inch giant whose many feats
included the "taming" of Andrew Jackson.

Coffee was a trusted officer under Jackson in the Indian wars and made a name for himself at the Battle of New Orleans. Later in life—at the age of thirty-seven—he married sixteen-year-old Mary Donelson, niece of Rachel Jackson.

In addition to his activities as a soldier and partner with Jackson in a store at Clover Bottom, Coffee was a surveyor of note, laying out, among others, the city of Huntsville, Alabama. When John Coffee died on July 7, 1833, at the age of sixty-one, General, then President, Jackson, wrote this epitaph:

"As a husband, parent and friend, he was affectionate, tender, and sincere. He was a brave, prompt, and skillful general; a distinguished and sagacious patriot; an unpretending, just and honest man . . . "

13

When Taft Came to Nashville

Through the years Nashville has had its share of famous visitors, and it has always been the custom to treat them royally. But no visitor was ever treated in a grander manner than was William Howard Taft back on May 21, 1908, when he came to Nashville to address the twenty-fifth annual convention of the Tennessee Bar Association.

His host was Jacob McGavock Dickinson, famous Nashville attorney, who had already served as Assistant Attorney General of the United States under President Grover Cleveland.

At the time of Taft's visit, Dickinson was General Counsel for the Illinois Central Railroad and resided in Chicago. However, he had purchased Belle Meade mansion and four hundred acres of land so he and his wife would have a place to stay when they visited Nashville. A son, John Overton Dickinson, and his family made their home at the mansion.

A great deal of planning went into preparing for the visit by Taft, at the time Secretary of War and only a few months away from becoming President of the United States. One problem was finding a bathtub large enough to accommodate the three-hundred-pound Taft, the largest person, incidentally, ever to serve as president. The problem was solved by installing a special bathtub in the quarters to which Secretary Taft would be assigned.

No one in Tennessee was better suited for entertaining presidents than was Jacob McGavock Dickinson. At a time when the ultimate luxury was simply to ride a pullman car on a train, Dickinson had his own private railway car, which he used for his frequent trips between Chicago and Nashville. A special siding was set up at the Belle Meade station to accommodate his car.

On the day of his visit, Taft rode to Belle Meade mansion in an open carriage with United States Supreme Court Justice H. H. Lurton, formerly of Nashville. A special train was arranged to take members of the bar from downtown Union Station to the estate.

As visitors disembarked at the Belle Meade station and walked up the tree-lined driveway to the mansion, they were greeted by the tolling of the plantation farm bell. The guests were served barbecued pork and lamb, as well as buttermilk from large coolers.

The following year, after Taft had become president, he named Dickinson Secretary of War; but their close personal relationship was probably not a factor. Dickinson was eminently qualified for the job.

After attending preparatory school at Montgomery Bell Academy, he had received Bachelor of Arts and Master of Arts degrees at Vanderbilt University. He studied law at Columbia University and followed this with study at the University of Leipzig and the Sorbonne in Paris.

He was admitted to the bar in 1874, opening a law office in Nashville. He was married to Martha Overton, daughter of Colonel John Overton and granddaughter of Judge John Overton of Travellers' Rest, a friend and promoter of Andrew Jackson.

After serving as Assistant United States Attorney for two years, Dickinson became general attorney for the Louisville and Nashville Railroad, serving also at the time as a professor of law at Vanderbilt.

Dickinson's most renowned national and international attention came in 1903 as a member of the Counsel for the

United States before the Alaskan Boundary Tribunal. His closing argument was generally regarded as central to the favorable solution of the dispute.

In December of that year the Chicago Bar Association honored Dickinson with a festive dinner. A telegram from President Theodore Roosevelt was read in which Roosevelt said of Dickinson's closing argument, "No cause of like importance was ever summed up in a more masterly manner than our cause was summed up by Judge Dickinson."

Dickinson, incidentally, had met Teddy Roosevelt two years earlier during a bear hunt in Mississippi.

Octavia Zollicoffer Bond, in a series of articles on leading Nashville families in the *Nashville Banner* of October 3, 1909, called Dickinson the "greatest living citizen of Nashville."

Certainly few Tennesseans ever had as many personal friends in high places as did Jacob McGavock Dickinson.

PART THREE:
Scenic Places

As this 1860 photograph shows, the state Capitol, on a high hill overlooking Nashville, had a majestic appearance from its earliest days.

14
The "Lost" State of Franklin

For four years the State of Franklin occupied a part of what is now Tennessee. Few realize how close it came to becoming a permanent state. Surely the "lost" State of Franklin occupies a unique position, not only in Tennessee, but in United States, history.

As one historian put it, "The situation was one without parallel in American jurisprudence, since Franklin was and is the only example of a *de facto* American state that functioned in every aspect of statal power."

Plans for the state were begun at a convention held in Jonesboro on August 23, 1784. Among those attending were such famous early pioneers as John Sevier, William Cocke, Colonel Arthur Campbell, and the Reverend Samuel Houston, uncle of the man who became governor of Tennessee, president of the Republic of Texas, then United States senator and governor of Texas.

Governed by Sevier, Franklin operated for four years in every way as a state, levying taxes and passing laws.

The term "lost" seems to have been coined by Samuel Cole Williams, a former justice of the Tennessee Supreme Court and author of the very excellent work, *History of the Lost State of Franklin* (The Press of the Pioneers, 1933).

The counties making up the state—Washington, Sullivan, Greene, and Hawkins (later subdivided to include the counties of Wayne, Caswell, Spencer, Sevier, and Blount)—were "lost" in the sense that they were at the time in a portion of North Carolina to the west of the Appalachian mountain range.

Their plight was not dissimilar to that of the American colonies of a decade earlier. Word of the defection of Franklin reached England and their case was well-stated in the British *Gentleman's Magazine* of August 1785: "The people of the western counties found themselves grievously taxed without enjoying the blessings of it."

After failing to gain the approval of the mother state, North Carolina, to form their own state, the Franklinites petitioned the Continental Congress for statehood, with William Cocke taking the petition to New York, where Congress was in session.

According to law, a two-thirds majority was needed—nine of the thirteen states. When the vote was taken, seven states voted aye, two short of the required number. North Carolina, being a party to the dispute, did not vote; and the two-man delegation from South Carolina was divided.

Judge Williams commented, "It is interesting to speculate on the fate of the new state had it been named 'Jefferson' instead of 'Franklin,' linked so to speak with a personality of abounding vigor and breadth of vision (Thomas Jefferson), to a rising rather than a setting sun (Benjamin Franklin)."

Jefferson would indeed have been the more politic name than Franklin. In addition to owning land in what was to become Tennessee, Jefferson had supported its petition for statehood and had predicted that it, along with Kentucky (then a part of Virginia), would win statehood. He was correct on the latter count; and the principal reason was that Virginia supported Kentucky statehood, while North Carolina, particularly its legislature and some of its governors, opposed statehood for Franklin.

Benjamin Franklin, on the other hand, upon being informed by Cocke that leaders of the state of Franklin wished to name it for him, wrote a warm letter in which he said he was honored. But he offered no practical assistance and declined an invitation to visit the area.

At its peak, about 1788, the state of Franklin had a population of some forty thousand. Governor Richard Caswell of North Carolina avoided sending an army to put down the rebellion for the very practical reason that his state troops would have had great difficulty subduing the long rifles of John Sevier and his men.

The decline of Franklin was due to a combination of circumstances. When the national government signed the Treaty of Hopewell with the Cherokees, two of the four commissioners were from North Carolina. One of those was Joseph Martin, who had been governor at the time of Franklin's beginning and had violently opposed it. Among other things, the treaty gave the Cherokees rights to a sizable part of the state of Franklin, including the recently designated permanent capital of Greeneville (replacing Jonesboro).

While the Franklinites ignored the treaty, this action by the national government had a weakening effect on the whole structure. About this time stories of the rich lands to the west were luring Franklin residents to leave the area, and the population slowly began to decline.

When people lost faith in Franklin's currency, an earlier custom of using furs in trade was revived. Public servants were paid in furs—the governor receiving one thousand deerskins as his annual salary, the chief justice five hundred deerskins, the secretary to the governor, five hundred raccoon skins, and the justice of the peace one muskrat skin for signing a warrant.

A few years later, Senator Daniel Webster was to commend the Franklinites in an address to Congress. "I am of the opinion," he said, "that, until Congress shall perform its duty by seeing that the country enjoys a good currency, the same medium which the people are obliged to use, whether it be skins or rags, is good for its own members."

15

Clarksville, the City That Wouldn't Die

The first settlers in the area of Clarksville, Middle Tennessee's second city, gave new meaning to the term "never say die." When death came to some, it meant that others would come to take their place. And they adhered to a maxim that was probably old even then—"If at first you don't succeed, try, try, again."

When long hunters (those who hunted for a year or more before returning to their homes) came into the area in the 1770s, some of them were impressed by the beauty of the countryside, the seeming fertility of the soil, and the abundance of wildlife. They dreamed of returning there at a later time to build their homes and settle down with their families.

Such a person was Moses Renfroe. He had noted a place where the Cumberland and the Red rivers joined, marked by tall bluffs with reddish-tinged rocks and appropriately called "Red Paint Hill."

Renfroe was present when the flotilla of some thirty flatboats, dugouts, and canoes led by John Donelson reached the Red Paint Hill landmark on April 12, 1780. Renfroe left the Donelson party that was to push on to French Lick (now Nashville).

With Renfroe were his family and the families of Joseph and James Renfroe and their relatives, Nathan and Solomon

Turpin, and a number of others. They proceeded up the Red River and settled at a point between what is now Clarksville and Port Royal.

What Renfroe and his people had not anticipated was the intense hostility that the Indians felt toward the white people who came with the notion of clearing off ground and raising crops. The flames of the Indians' resentment were fanned by the Spanish government.

The Treaty of Paris, ending the Revolutionary War, had left Spain in control of the mouth and the west bank of the Mississippi River. Spain did not like the idea of the settlers coming into the Cumberland area and sought to force their evacuation by uniting the Indians against them. Some historians say that Spain even paid a bounty for white scalps.

Meanwhile, Moses Renfroe was joined by others, the families of Isaac Renfroe, Isaac Mayfield, James Hollis, James Johns, and Abraham Jones.

Less than three months after Moses arrived, Indians went on the attack. Among the victims were Joseph Renfroe, Abraham Jones, and a number of others who were not identified. Devastated by their tragedy, the surviving settlers abandoned their homes and never returned.

Meanwhile, other settlements were being made along the Cumberland; and in 1784 John Montgomery, a long hunter of the 1770s, and Martin Armstrong chose a site on the eastern side of the Cumberland River just south of the junction of the Cumberland and the Red rivers. There Armstrong laid out the town that would be called Clarksville.

It was named for George Rogers Clark, the Revolutionary War leader and a colleague of Montgomery. The county in which Clarksville was located would later be named for Montgomery.

Other settlers continued moving into the area. Many were killed. But the settlers kept coming. Montgomery himself was killed in 1794, just ten years after he had helped found Clarksville.

Of the spirit of the early Clarksville settlers, Charles M.

Waters, author of *Historic Clarksville: The Bicentennial Story, 1784-1984*, wrote:

> "Man does not give up easily. He is a resilient and restless creature responding to the magnetic attraction of two invisible forces, one of which is the lodestone of migration ever pulling him from where he is to what he hopes will be a better place. At the same time, man is drawn by another force, that of the love of the land which makes him want to stop and settle down."

Tragic indeed was the story of Valentine Sevier, who moved from Nashville to the New Providence area around 1790. It should be noted that Valentine Sevier was a brother of John Sevier who, in addition to his service as governor of the state of Franklin and of Tennessee and as a member of Congress, was noted for his exploits as an Indian fighter. In spite of numerous battles with the Indians and various military engagements such as the Battle of King's Mountain, John Sevier seemingly led a charmed life and reached the ripe old age of seventy. He also reared seventeen children to maturity.

Valentine Sevier had an untimely death because of tragedy that befell his family. His son-in-law, Thomas Grantham, was killed by Indians in October 1791 while hunting near Sevier's Station. The following January three of Sevier's sons were killed. In 1794 another Indian attack was made on the Sevier Station and his two daughters, Elizabeth and Ann, Elizabeth's husband, Charles Snyder, Sevier's six-year-old son, Joseph, and two of his grandchildren were killed.

Sevier's twelve-year-old daughter Rebecca was scalped, but she recovered. Thus over a period of three years Sevier lost four sons, two daughters, and two sons-in-law, along with several grandchildren. His livestock was stolen and his station burned, with the exception of his stone house, which still stands.

Sevier moved what was left of his family to Nashville, but he returned to Clarksville in 1796. Four years later he died, a broken and broken-hearted man. He was buried on his own property across the river from his abandoned station. The site later became a cemetery.

In 1795 Clarksville and the entire region greatly benefited from Thomas Pinckney's treaty with the Spanish and the Indians. The warfare, for all practical purposes, ceased.

During the entire year of 1984, Clarksville celebrated its bicentennial with a full calendar of events. The first occurred on a bitterly cold day, January 16, the two-hundredth anniversary of the purchase of the site for the city by John Montgomery and Martin Armstrong.

A re-enactment of the arrival in 1780 by flatboat of the party of settlers led by Moses Renfroe was held April 14, 1984. An official Homecoming Day was held in June. Among the dignitaries taking part was United States Army Chief of Staff General John A. Wickham, Jr., former commander of the 101st Airborne Division at nearby Fort Campbell. There was dancing at Dunbar Cave to music of the "Big Band" era and a performance by Roy Acuff and his Smoky Mountain Boys. Clarksville, a city of 55,000 population, had indeed come a long way since its modest and tragic beginnings.

16

The Building of Tennessee's Capitol

When William Strickland, the noted Philadelphia architect, came to Nashville in 1845 to plan and direct the building of the State Capitol, he fully expected to be finished with the job in two or three years. Little did he realize that he would stay for nine years and still not live to see the project finished. Perhaps if he could have foreseen some of the difficulties he would face, the haranguing and the criticism he would receive, he might never have left the "City of Brotherly Love."

But William Strickland was a dedicated man, and the colorful statehouse sitting atop one of Nashville's highest hills is a monument to his skill and devotion.

The land for the site, totaling about four acres, was donated by the city of Nashville. Initially, the city bought property from Judge George W. Campbell for $30,000 and added more later at an additional cost of $42,150. It is said that Judge Campbell obtained the land originally for the price of a cow and calf. He had sold the cow and calf to a farmer on credit. Later, the farmer informed him he was unable to pay, and so he gave the judge the land and a gun instead.

Erection of the Capitol was a monumental task. The sums of money involved, while chicken feed in terms of the cost of today's office buildings, staggered the imaginations of the legislators of that period. At one point when the General Assembly was debating a $200,000 appropriation, one legislator proposed that it be cut to $10,000, declaring that sum adequate to complete the building, "whitewash it and put a fence around it." But there were forward-looking and progressive men in the government, and their will prevailed, although legislative appropriations came slowly and in small sums, resulting in continuing delays in getting the job done.

One money-saving device suggested by Strickland, and which was approved by the Legislature, was the use of labor from the State Penitentiary. An estimated $100,000 was saved by the use of from 100 to 120 prisoners throughout the time of the project. Their job was primarily to work in quarries cutting the large chunks of limestone used in the building. Stone masons and other skilled labor were also used. There was much criticism of using prison labor, particularly from "mechanics" (the word had a different usage then) who felt it to be an invasion of their domain.

Strickland's salary was a modest $2,500 a year and part of it was withheld and paid his widow only after his death. His son, Francis, worked for him for five years at a stipulated salary of eighty dollars a month before collecting a penny of it.

The Capitol was sufficiently well along to allow the Legislature to meet in its chambers by October 1853. Strickland died on April 7, 1854, six weeks after the Legislature had passed an act setting up a vault as a burial place for him "in honor of his genius in erecting so grand a work." Strickland himself had chosen the exact place of his entombment—at the northeast wall of the north basement portico. Samuel Morgan, the only member of the Capitol commission to serve the entire time of its building, was also buried in the Capitol.

On Saturday, April 8, 1854, the *Nashville True Whig* carried a brief announcement of Strickland's death at the City Hotel, where he had been a "citizen boarder" for several years. On April 20, 1854, the Board of Commissioners adopted resolutions calling for payment of the remainder of

Strickland's salary still owing him to his widow and for his funeral expenses, the latter totaling $108.

His son was chosen to direct completion of the Capitol. In a final report, the Board placed the total cost at $508,565.47.

17
Rock City Magic

While thousands of people went broke during the Great Depression and others took out their frustrations by jumping off high buildings, yet others seized on ideas for giving the public something for its scarce and hard-earned dollars and made millions in the process.

One such was a native of Sweetwater, Tennessee, Garnet Carter. He masterminded and promoted what came to be viewed by some as the eighth wonder of the world, Rock City.

Carter, who had traveled the United States as a "drummer," or salesman, eventually settled with his wife Frieda in the Lookout Mountain area near Chattanooga. Carter, with his associate, O. B. Andrews, went into real estate on a large scale, taking out options on three hundred acres of property atop the mountain.

This occurred in the late 1920s, and as the Depression arrived the real estate business slowed to a crawl. But Garnet and Frieda Carter had one little ace in the hole. They had kept for themselves a ten-acre plot from the edge of which one could have a spectacular view of a wide expanse of the valley.

During the time that Mr. Carter worked on real estate deals, Mrs. Carter had chosen some of the rockiest parts of the home plot for a garden. Observing its pathways through narrow passages of rocky walls, its trickling mountain streams, and the beauty of the scene in the valley below, the idea struck her, "Why not make the garden into a tourist attraction?"

Her husband, a natural-born promoter, agreed it was worth a try. They began working on the idea in 1930, and Rock City officially opened in 1932. There was Lover's Leap, so named, according to legend, for an Indian princess who jumped to her death on the jagged rocks below after learning that her brave had been unfaithful.

Near Lover's Leap was an area from which, according to the owners, one could view parts of seven states. Large telescopes, with slots for coins to be deposited by viewers, helped make the claim believable.

The main attraction, then and now, was the walk one could take through massive rocks, fissures, pits, and caverns, over dizzily suspended bridges (stationary bridges for the faint-hearted) and down through a wonderland for children. There little fairies, in gaily colored attire, go about their activities, thrilling the young and the young at heart as well.

From the start, Garnet Carter knew that Rock City was blessed by an ideal location. It lay alongside the main route from the entire eastern half of the United States to Florida. His job, then, was to let the millions of tourists passing his way know of Rock City and of its easy accessibility.

This he accomplished by one of the most unusual and effective campaigns in the annals of advertising. The most visible part of that campaign was one in which the Rock City message was proclaimed from the tops of thousands of barns along twelve thousand miles of highway in eighteen states. The message was simple and direct: "See Rock City," or such variations as "It Would Be a Pity To Miss Rock City" and "See Rock City Atop Lookout Mountain Chattanooga."

Clark Byers, a friend of Carter's, had the job of painting the signs on the barns and keeping them in a highly visible state of repair. Byers was on the road constantly painting two barns a day, or about four hundred a year.

Farmers were paid from five to fifteen dollars and, more important, got a free paint job for their barns. Another highly

From Rock City's Lover's Leap, visitors can get a breathtaking view of the valley below and the Great Smoky Mountains in the distance while listening to the roar of a 90-foot waterfall.

successful part of the ad campaign was the production of thousands of little bird houses proclaiming "See Rock City." They were placed near motels, campgrounds, and in many other spots where tourists could not miss seeing them.

At the peak of the campaign, some eight hundred barns were in use. In more recent times, the development of interstate highways, with their advertising restrictions, has made the barn technique less practical.

But this has not cramped the style of those who carry on the Rock City tradition. One alternative has been a hot-air balloon bearing the Rock City slogan traveling around the country for public events and balloon races. And millions of brochures have been printed for distribution to prospective visitors and to those who visit the site.

Those who go to Rock City and leave their cars parked for even a short time will find a bumper sticker affixed to the rear bumper bearing the message, "We Saw Rock City."

The state of Tennessee, meanwhile, has recognized that the millions who have trekked to Rock City for over a half-century have made a substantial contribution to other businesses and to its own tax coffers.

It is thus understandable that when legislation was proposed in the Tennessee General Assembly to exempt from the Beautification Act of 1965 such landmarks of "nostalgic or historical value" as the existing barn-side advertising of Rock City, it was approved without dissent.

Probably the ultimate compliment paid to Rock City and its owners is the recognition it has won among newspaper editorial cartoonists. A cartoon in the *Atlanta Constitution* showed the barren landscape of Mars broken only by a Rock City birdhouse. Another, in the Augusta (Georgia) *Chronicle Herald*, appearing shortly after Jimmy Carter's inauguration, showed the White House with one end painted "See Rock City" and a voice balloon from inside saying, "Billy, you've just gotta come up for a visit. You just won't believe how much it looks like home already."

18

The Mystery of the Old Stone Fort

Picture if you can a man-made "fort" dating back to the time of Jesus Christ. Near Manchester, Tennessee, is an elaborate project carried out by intelligent human beings almost fifteen hundred years before Columbus arrived on the scene, one thousand years before Leif Ericson is believed to have made his voyage to North America.

Naturally, some impressive tales have been told concerning who built the "fort," for what purposes, and some of the trials they faced during those early times. We'll mention some of those stories and theories, but the most interesting one of all is what archaeologists believe to have really happened.

First, a few facts. The Old Stone Fort is not a fort in the sense you would expect. It is not built of hewn logs such as you will find at Fort Nashborough in Nashville. It is an enclosure of rock and earth walls, impressive in size and engineering and built on a natural plateau covering fifty-four acres, where the Big and the Little Duck rivers converge.

Bluffs from sixty to one hundred feet high form natural barriers on two sides of the enclosure. The man-made walls, on the north and south, cross the neck of land between the forks and terminate where the bluffs afford natural barriers. The south wall alone stretches 2,111 feet from one stream to

the other, attesting to the size of the project that was undertaken by the builders.

The walls, where they still exist, range from three to six
feet high and have a total length of some 4,600 feet. By today's standards, the construction of such walls would be no
great accomplishment. Bulldozers, dump trucks, cranes,
and dynamite would make the gathering and movement of
earth and stone quite simple. But two thousand years ago, it
was far different. Imagine the immense task of carrying
rocks, some weighing as much as seventy pounds, up the
steep bluffs from the river, and carrying thousands of tons of
earth to the walls—not in dump trucks but in baskets.

And now a few theories.

There is, for instance, the Welsh (Madoc) Theory as told by
Basil B. McMahan in *The Mystery of the Old Stone Fort* (Tennessee Book Co., 1965). He recounts legends in Wales that
tell of Madoc, the son of Own of Gwyneth, who about 1170
A.D. left the craggy highland of his homeland and "sailed
west" to an unknown land. According to the story, Madoc
reached what is now known as Mobile Bay. Some of his party
went by river and overland to the vicinity of the Old Stone
Fort.

Other stories tell of white settlers who came long before
Madoc, Ericson, or Columbus. It is believed that they found it
necessary to build the fort because their crossbows were no
match for the bows and arrows of hostile Indians. To substan-
tiate their theory that the fort was built by early white settlers,
some theorists note that various early settlers, including John
Sevier and Francis Lewis, one of the signers of the Declaration of Independence, wrote of encounters with Indians "re-
markably white" with hair of a "reddish color."

Our knowledge of the fort and its origins greatly expanded
in 1966 when excavations of the enclosed area were conducted by an archaeological team from the University of Tennessee. Among the participants was Dr. Charles H. Faulkner,
who wrote a detailed report of their findings.

While many of their discoveries tended to debunk some of

the existing theories—for instance, what was thought to have been a "moat" near the fort was actually the old river bed of the Big Duck River, which over the years had changed its course—their findings tended to confirm that the fort was indeed built two thousand years ago, and that it took the builders four hundred years to do it!

The archaeological team arrived at the date of construction by the radiocarbon (carbon 14) technique for dating charcoal samples found in the rock-filled walls. Four samples were submitted to Geochron Laboratories, Inc., of Cambridge, Massachusetts, for dating. The age of one sample was dated at 1,920 years, "give or take 85 years," or an approximate date of 30 A.D. The dates of the other samples ranged from 220 to 430 A.D., lending credence to the claim it took possibly as much as four hundred years to build the fort.

On the basis of their findings, the archaeologists also reached the conclusion that the walls were built by prehistoric Indians, identified as Middle Woodland Indians, not white immigrants.

While the team conceded that the actual purpose of the fort remained a mystery, they tended to discount theories that it was used for military purposes. They leaned more to the idea that it was used as a ceremonial site, as a means by which the builders could make peace with their gods.

The old fort has served several uses since the passing of its prehistoric inhabitants. During Manchester's early days, water powered mills along the banks of the Duck River were used for industrial purposes. During the Civil War, three hundred Union troops were stationed within the boundaries of the fort. Today it is part of a 940-acre tract operated by the Tennessee Department of Conservation.

There are fifty-one developed campsites, a primitive camping area, and a nearby nine-hole golf course. A visitors' center, a museum with exhibits relating most of the legends and factual data known about the site, fishing, picnicking, and hiking are available.

19
Abraham Lincoln's Dream Come True

Many Tennesseans have never heard of a small town in the Cumberland Gap area called Harrogate, and fewer still know that the college there is a living memorial to Abraham Lincoln.

The way that Lincoln Memorial University came into being would strain the imagination of a good fiction writer.

The time was September of 1863, and the place was the White House. General Oliver Otis Howard, a close friend of President Lincoln and one of his most trusted generals, was at the White House to discuss military strategy for pursuing the Civil War in the Cumberland Gap area.

General Howard later reported that as they pored over a map of the region, the president pointed to it and said, "General, if you come out of this horror and misery alive, and I hope that you may, I want you to do something for these people who have been shut out of the world all these years. If I live, I will do all I can to aid you, and between us we may do them the justice they deserve. Please remember, and if God is good to us, we may be able to speak of it later."

It would be many years before the general got his opportunity, but he never forgot his chief's words. When the chance finally came, like any good general he seized the opportunity and pressed toward his goal with vigor and determination.

*   *   *   *   *   *   *   *

The Civil War was still raging when the Reverend and Mrs. Arthur A. Myers went to Kentucky under the auspices of the American Missionary Association. A Congregational minister, the Reverend Myers had devoted his entire life to the goal of "bringing the teachings of God and man to the people of Appalachia."

The Myers spent many years in Kentucky's Appalachia, holding prayer meetings and organizing elementary schools. The need was great, for during the economic decline that followed the Civil War, many private schools failed and tax-supported public education was not yet widespread.

In 1888 the Reverend Myers received a call to Cumberland Gap. Within two years he had solicited the necessary funds for a new church; Mrs. Myers opened a school in the church's basement. Two years later, the Cumberland Gap Hotel became vacant, and the ever-enterprising preacher raised the necessary funds for a high school. It was to be named Harrow, for the British school.

With tuition at a reasonable—even for that day and time—rate of one dollar per month, the school's single building, Harrow Hall, was soon overflowing with 255 mountain youth. Then the hard times settled in, and enrollment was down to one hundred by 1895.

The time was ripe for the appearance of General Howard. In June of that year the Reverend Myers heard that General Howard planned to be in East Tennessee to talk on the Battle of Chattanooga. Through the general's son, Captain Henry S. Howard, he invited General Howard to address Harrow Academy's graduating class. The general accepted; and after his stirring talk on Grant at Chattanooga, he and several influential friends were invited to the Myers' home for dinner.

At the proper moment—probably after dinner when everyone was in a relaxed mood (the preacher was a skilled promoter)—the Reverend Myers brought up the sad plight of his school and appealed for help. As the story goes, the general began pacing back and forth. From where he walked, he could see the historic Cumberland Gap, where the states of Tennessee, Virginia, and Kentucky join, soil once trod by Daniel Boone and by Thomas and Nancy Hanks Lincoln on their way to Kentucky, where their famous son was born.

It had been just short of thirty-two years since the general had met the president in the White House, but he still remembered those words as if they had just been spoken: "I want you to do something for these people who have been shut out of the world all these years."

Suddenly the general stopped his pacing and said, "Friends, if you will make this school a larger enterprise, I will take hold and do what I can."

It was decided, upon the general's suggestion, to charter a university to be named Lincoln Memorial University. It would operate as a living memorial to the sixteenth president of the United States. The minister did not waste any time in drawing up a charter and finding a charter committee, which later became the university's Board of Trustees.

Its charter provided that in addition to being a memorial to Abraham Lincoln, the purpose of the university was to serve as "an expression of renewed good will and fraternal feelings between the people of sections of this country once opposed to each other in civil war . . . (that it would) impart instruction in the various branches of education, science, art and industry. . . ." It stated further that the university would be "for the glory of God and the advancement of brotherhood among men: and said university shall ever seek to make education possible to the children of the humble, common people of America, among whom Abraham Lincoln was born, and whom he said God must love because he made so many of them."

The university was chartered on Lincoln's eighty-eighth birthday, February 12, 1897. In keeping with the goal of bringing all the people together, its first major building, a three-hundred-foot structure that had been a sanatorium, was named Grant-Lee Hall.

General Howard then set out to obtain nationwide support

for the institution. He brought in national figures to serve on the board, among whom was the slain president's son, Robert Todd Lincoln.

At a celebration of Lincoln's birthday in 1901 in Carnegie Hall—where Mark Twain was the master of ceremonies—General Howard explained the origin and purposes of the university. The event was reported the following day in the *New York Times*, and after that contributions began to flow. Among presidents who took an interest in it were Theodore Roosevelt, William Howard Taft, and Woodrow Wilson.

Lincoln Memorial has had its ups and downs, but it is still a thriving university. Enrollment, which dropped (from 750 in the late '60s) to 517 in 1973, is now up to almost 1,500. Its students pursue thirty-four types of undergraduate and three types of graduate degrees. Most are from Kentucky, Tennessee, and Virginia; but some come from as far away as Japan.

The university still lives up to its purpose as stated in the charter: to serve the common people. A full third of its students come from households in which family incomes are below $6,000, and one-half are from families earning less than $9,000 per year. More than three of every four are among the first generation in their families to attend college.

Over the years, the university has amassed one of the most complete Lincoln/Civil War collections in America (second only to the state collection in Illinois). The Abraham Lincoln Museum annually attracts more than fifty thousand visitors to the campus.

20

The Fascinating Caves of Tennessee

Tennessee has an abundance of caves. With more than seven hundred of them in seventy-four counties of the eastern and middle areas of the state, Tennessee probably possesses the largest concentration of caves anywhere in the world.

The most famous of the Volunteer State's caves is Ruby Falls. Its attraction as a tourist spot is enhanced by its proximity to Rock City on Lookout Mountain just outside the city of Chattanooga. Those who visit Ruby Falls with her sparkling stalagmites and stalactites and awe-inspiring falls learn of its enchanting history. For many years only the Indians knew the location of the entrance to the cave. Later the falls were discovered after white explorers dug through to the cave from another place.

Tennessee's largest cave—and America's second largest (behind Kentucky's Mammoth Cave)—is Cumberland Caverns, located just off Highway 70 South near McMinnville. Then there are other such caves as Tuckaleechee—greatest sight under the Smokies—Mirror Lake, the Hall of Dreams, and Onyx Jungle, all, along with Ruby Falls, a part of the Lookout Mountain Caves, and Craighead Caverns with its Lost Sea.

Tennessee's caves have colorful histories, part factual and

part legendary. Frequently it is hard to know where the true stories end and the fiction begins.

Certainly caves have served useful purposes for centuries. Cumberland Caverns, for instance, along with a number of others, was used as a Confederate rendezvous during the Civil War. Nitrate has been mined from it as well.

Meredith Cave in Campbell County was once used by the entire community as a storage place for fruits and vegetables (most caves have temperatures in the fifty-degree range), and there is evidence that the use of caves as burial grounds is not confined entirely to the ancient past. Many Tennessee caves are suited for plays, restaurants, and dance floors. During Prohibition, some caves were converted to thriving speakeasies.

Dunbar Cave near Clarksville has been the source of a number of stories. One concerns an incident during the heyday of Jesse James and his brother Frank. According to the story, the James boys escaped from a sheriff's posse by fleeing into Dunbar Cave.

Confident that there was no other exit from the cave, the posse stationed itself outside the entrance and waited for the desperadoes to emerge. Imagine their embarrassment a few days later when the Jameses were spotted elsewhere, having uncovered an exit that no one else to this day has found.

Visitors to Dunbar Cave have been shown "Independence Hall," where Jenny Lind once sang and, at a point fifteen hundred feet from the cave's entrance, "Peterson's Leap." The "Leap" is a thirty-five-foot pit that, according to tradition, claimed the life of a man named Peterson after he became lost and fell into the hole.

Then there's the story of Aaron Higginbotham, the surveyor who discovered Cumberland Caverns in 1810. It seems that Higginbotham entered the cave alone one night and, guided by the light from a flickering torch, sought to explore its depths. Suddenly his torch burned out, leaving him stranded on a high ledge in the terrifying darkness of the cave. Rescuers found him several days later in the same spot "his hair turned snow white from the ordeal."

In Cannon County, Devil's Hole Cave is so named because, according to one source, "For nearly a hundred years the Devil's Hole has been the center of local rumor and legend, and more than one missing person is supposed to have vanished into its depths."

Possibly the cave story that "takes the cake" comes from Cumberland Mountain Saltpeter Cave in Claiborne County. Our source reports a "strange phenomenon, which certain residents of the area attest to having observed—on damp nights a series of lights is said to emerge from the cave, travel rapidly to the top of the mountain along the crest, and back again."

A guide explaining our caves to a group of visitors would be quite correct in saying that the caves have been around "longer than we have." According to a brochure telling of the Lost Sea and Craighead Caverns, caves date back more than three hundred million years. Thomas C. Barr, Jr., author of a book on Tennessee caves published by the Tennessee Department of Conservation, Division of Geology, dates caves according to era. Some may be Cretaceous (primitive mammals and the last of the dinosaurs); most are not much older than Pliocene, and some are perhaps Pleistocene. That means that most of them probably date back to the time of the more advanced animals and plants, but before man appeared on the scene.

Despite many hair-raising stories about caves, most of them, especially the commercially operated ones, are well-lighted and practically hazard-free.

PART FOUR

Indian Tales

An artist's conception of the dogs that repulsed an Indian attack on Fort Nashborough.

Photo courtesy of James A. Crutchfield

21

Dogs Save the Day at Fort Nashborough

Few stories in history can compare with that of the hardy band that stuck it out with Captain James Robertson in the early years at Fort Nashborough.

Putnam in his *History of Middle Tennessee* paints this grim picture:

"As the winter of 1781–2 approached with rains, snow and sleet, the apprehension of destitution and suffering among the stationers was very great. They had endured much in the two years of settlement, or imprisonment and siege, as their condition may more properly be called.

"They had seen the majority of original adventurers depart (including Colonel John Donelson, an event comparable to Moses taking leave of the Hebrew people in the middle of the wilderness); they had seen yet sadder and more discouraging sights than such desertion—a large proportion of their small band stricken down and savagely mangled by enemies still lurking around and far outnumbering the whites. They had been enabled to cultivate, gather, and house but a small supply of provender for their cattle, or food for themselves."

But because they possessed "a strange contempt of hardships and exposures, a fearlessness, love of adventure, and determined perseverance," they stayed.

It was through an odd combination of circumstances that the pre-Nashville pioneers had such a hard time of it. At first, it appeared they had indeed found a Promised Land. The Indians seemed peaceful, and there was a bountiful supply of game.

This caused the settlers to waste their ammunition on game; and after the Indians turned hostile, they had precious little of it left. Before the end of the first year after that historic arrival on Christmas Day, 1779, open warfare existed between the settlers and the Indians. The Indians would ambush the unwary who journeyed into the wilderness to hunt, or for whatever reason. They would shoot the settlers as they tried to work in the fields. Another favorite sport was to scare game away from the vicinity of the fort, forcing the pioneers to venture farther afield. Thus the pioneers became prime targets for the arrows and rifle balls of the Indians. Still another trick was to shoot the cattle of the settlers and to steal their horses.

As in all such trying times, there were moments of heroism, events which the lonely pioneers could recall during long winter evenings before a blazing fire in an open hearth of the sturdy fort. Mrs. James Robertson's favorite was the "Battle of the Bluffs," an event which the Indians carefully planned and almost successfully executed.

During the night of April 1, 1781, a large party of Cherokees set up an ambush some distance from the fort. During the early morning hours, three of them approached the fort, fired their guns and ran away. Impulsive and perhaps a little foolhardy, twenty of the pioneers, led by Captain Robertson himself, mounted their horses and gave chase. Too late, they discovered that they had been lured into a trap. With the Indians firing at them from every direction, they dismounted and returned the fire.

Frightened by the gunfire, the horses bolted, leaving their riders on foot. A line of Indians moved in to cut off their return to the fort. At this critical moment, it appeared the settlers would be mowed down like an Ivy League defensive line. But Mama Robertson was not finished. She unleashed a pack of fifty fierce dogs, all of them sharing their owners' dislike for their Indian foes. Their fierce onslaught upon the enemy, plus the commotion stirred up by the stampeding horses, created the necessary diversion to permit most of the pioneers to return to the fort.

After their return, one pious mother was heard to say, "Thanks be to God, that he gave Indians a fear of dogs and a love of horses."

Among those in the thick of the battle were the Castleman brothers—Abraham, Andrew, Joseph, Hans, and Jacob. When two of them were killed by the enemy, Abe, who was called the "fool warrior" by the Indians, organized a party to track down their attackers. Seven of the boldest, including Abe, followed them across the Tennessee River near the present Nickajack Dam, adorned themselves with Indian dress and warpaint, and defeated a hunting party of 50. They returned with another tale to tell during the long nights at Fort Nashborough.

22
Sequoyah's Dream

Growing up in a small Cherokee village on the Little Tennessee River of East Tennessee, Sequoyah, a precocious half-Indian lad, was fascinated with the way white men made marks on "leaves" (paper) and then made the marks "talk" back to them.

He would be past the age of forty before his dream came true, but he never lost sight of it—to fashion an alphabet incorporating all the sounds of the Cherokee language so his people could read from their own "leaves."

Sequoyah was the son of a Cherokee woman and a white British trader named Nathaniel Gist. Gist abandoned Sequoyah's mother shortly after he was born, and so Sequoyah helped with her small dairy while he was a youth. Later he became skilled at silver-working and blacksmithing, opening a trading post of his own.

Sequoyah eventually expanded his trading establishment into a tavern and became a victim of the spirits he sold to his guests. Concerned by his often drunken state, a friend by the name of George Lowrey took Sequoyah in hand and persuaded him to sign—and keep—a temperance pledge.

Sequoyah, whose date of birth is placed by some as early as 1760, did not begin his language project until 1809. He perfected it twelve years later. He divided all the syllables of the spoken Cherokee language into eighty-six sounds, then came up with symbols to represent each of those sounds. Although he never learned to read or write the white man's language, he adapted many of the letters for his own alphabet from the English, turning some of them on their sides and others upside down.

Once his phonetic alphabet, or syllabary, was perfected, Sequoyah found it amazingly easy to teach it to others. His first pupil was his five-year-old daughter. Then he taught it to friends and acquaintances.

Convincing the Cherokees proved more difficult. His old friend George Lowrey agreed to ask the National Council of the Cherokees to give Sequoyah an opportunity to "sell" his language art to them. A group of young chiefs was sent to give him a hearing. After just seven days, the young men learned to read and write "Cherokee!" They proudly presented him to the Council, and his invention was officially proclaimed the national Cherokee language syllabary.

The language spread rapidly. Within a few months several thousand Cherokees had learned to read and write the symbols and were teaching others. They used it to write letters, to keep records, and, later on, to write their own constitution.

Then the National Council decided to publish a newspaper. In 1825 they purchased a printing press and, with help from white missionaries, began to print the *Cherokee Phoenix*, a weekly that was printed in both English and Cherokee.

Appearance of the newspaper brought Sequoyah's amazing accomplishment to the outside world. He was invited to Washington in 1828, and Congress voted him a gift of five hundred dollars in acknowledgment of his accomplishment. The Cherokee nation gave him a medal.

It was discovered, meanwhile, that Sequoyah's language could be adapted to other Indian dialects, and he went west to the Oklahoma Territory to help teach it to the various tribes there.

Sequoyah died in Mexico in 1843 while searching for lost Cherokee Indians. In recognition of his contributions to its early development, the state of Oklahoma chose him as one of

Sequoyah proudly displays his Cherokee alphabet.

its two representatives in Statuary Hall in the national capital. His home near Sallisaw, Oklahoma, stands as a memorial to him. In further recognition of his accomplishments, his name was given to the Giant Sequoia trees of California and to Sequoia National Park in that state.

23

The Indian Who Gave His Life for His Friends

The year was 1838. United States soldiers under General Winfield Scott were rounding up thousands of Indians throughout the Cherokee nation for the long twelve-hundred-mile trek through the heartland of America from North Carolina to Oklahoma.

Students of history were to call it, for good reason, "The Trail of Tears." Among those for whom the soldiers came was an aging Indian farmer, Tsali, and his elderly wife. The couple, their two sons, Ridges and Wasituna, and Tsali's brother-in-law, Lowney, were taken by two of Scott's soldiers from their cabin in the Great Smoky Mountains and marched down toward the valley, where a stockade awaited them.

As the small entourage walked along a narrow, winding mountain path, Tsali's wife stumbled and one of the soldiers prodded her with a bayonet, telling her to move along. The unprovoked attack angered Tsali, and he conceived a plan to escape. Speaking in Cherokee, which the soldiers did not understand, he told his kinsmen how he would fall as if he had injured his ankle and they would take the soldiers' guns.

As they reached a turn in the trail, Tsali suddenly fell to the ground, clutching his foot and yelling as if in pain. One of the soldiers rushed to him, and Ridges and Lowney grappled with the other soldier. Tsali grabbed the first soldier's foot, and he fell to the ground, dropping his rifle.

According to the Cherokees' story, the gun went off accidentally; but the bullet struck the soldier in the head and killed him instantly. The other soldier, meanwhile, escaped into the woods, leaving his gun with Tsali's kinsman. So the Indian group turned around and returned to the mountain wilderness.

Word of the soldier's death spread quickly, and General Scott vowed to capture the perpetrator of the crime. Meanwhile, the roundup continued. Cherokees were gathered into stockades for the mass exodus of 17,000 Indians to Oklahoma.

But other Cherokees, estimated at more than a thousand, continued to hide out in the mountains, including Tsali and his kin. Then the general had an idea. He would make Tsali and his family pay for their crime, but he would abandon his search for the others.

Scott used Will Thomas, a white trader who was the adopted son of an Indian couple, as a go-between. Thomas knew where Tsali was hiding, and he passed Scott's word to Tsali. If he and his kin would pay the penalty for their deed —death—Scott would have the government grant permission to the remaining Cherokees to remain in the Great Smokies.

When informed of the proposal, Tsali did not hesitate. "I will come," he said. He and his wife, his brother-in-law, and two sons, went to the stockade, where they were quickly executed. It is doubtful that any consideration was given during the brief trial as to whether the gun that killed the soldier was fired accidentally or not. The soldier was dead, and those who were responsible for his death must pay the price.

There was an element of mercy in the verdict, however. Tsali's wife and the younger son, Wasituna, were spared. Tsali, Ridges, and Lowney were sentenced to die before a firing squad. A colonel asked the old man if he had any last request. He replied, "If I must be killed, I would like to be shot by my own people."

Guns were given three Cherokee men, and they carried out

the order. Tsali and the other two were buried near the stockade. The area has since been covered by Lake Fontana.

Wasituna and his mother returned to their mountain home. His descendants still live on the Qualla Reservation in North Carolina, a sixty-five thousand acre expanse of which Cherokee is the capital. Thanks to the noble deed of Tsali, the Cherokee remnant remained, and their descendants carry on profitable activities that attract thousands of tourists each year.

One of the most popular attractions is an outdoor drama that has been staged during the summer season each year since 1950. Called *Unto These Hills,* it tells the story of the Cherokee Indians dating back to Hernando de Soto's arrival in 1540. Included is the dramatic role of Tsali and his family. More than four million persons have witnessed the story.

PART FIVE

Military Adventures

Native of Nashville
Who Gained Fame
As
Soldier of Fortune

WILLIAM WALKER, born in
Nashville, who proclaimed of Nicaragua
ragua and was executed by the
Honduran government at Trux-
illo(stone), Sept. 12, 1860.
He was known as "The Grey
Eyed Man of Destiny."

Courtesy Nashville Banner

WHERE WALKER WAS BORN.
The birthplace and boyhood home
of Walker on Fourth avenue was
razed in the opening of Commerce
street.

William Walker and the house where he was born on Fourth
Avenue in Nashville.

Photo courtesy the State Library and Archives

24

The "Gray-Eyed Man of Destiny"

They don't have his statue on the State Capitol grounds and the history books didn't allot him much space, but Nashville-born William Walker, the "gray-eyed man of destiny" made a big splash on the Central American scene around 1860. He most certainly would have altered the course of history if he had realized his grandiose scheme.

Small of stature—five feet, five inches—and possessed of an indomitable spirit, Walker had many of the characteristics of Napoleon. That he failed in his attempt to take over five Central American countries takes nothing away from the fact that he did indeed become the undisputed ruler of Nicaragua, first as commander-in-chief of the armed forces and later as "El Presidente."

Walker was a shining example of the dashing, daring filibusters of the period. Before the days of Huey Long and Theodore G. Bilbo, a filibuster was a freebooter or soldier of fortune who aided a revolution in a foreign country. *Webster's New Collegiate Dictionary* still gives this definition ahead of the more recent meaning—one who seeks to delay the legislative process through continuous speechmaking.

As a quiet lad growing up in Nashville, William Walker was a timid, shy, "mama's boy." He was quite a scholar, finishing well-respected Nashville University at the age of fourteen and later completing the necessary subjects to qualify himself as both a lawyer and a physician. He also had a knack for writing, working on newspapers in both New Orleans and San Francisco.

It was in New Orleans that he met the one and only love of his life—Helen Martin, described as being "so beautiful in face and character that her friends forgot the fact that she was both deaf and dumb." These weaknesses seemed to endear her all the more to him, and her untimely death shortly before they were to be wed was believed to have been the catalyst that launched his career as a soldier of fortune.

It was during the California Gold Rush of the late 1840s and early 50s that Walker went West, but gold was not his primary object. He wanted new worlds to conquer; and when it became evident that the United States frontier had been extended as far west as land would allow, he turned his eyes southward.

His first big crusade was to lead a band of forty-five men into Mexico and attempt to capture the states of Lower California and Sonora. Some have compared him to Don Quixote, but he at least gained valuable experience for his next exploit—Central America.

Walker's entry into Nicaragua was backed by powerful business interests, including Cornelius Vanderbilt, owner of a transportation line. Vanderbilt wanted political stability in Nicaragua because at that time the quickest route from New York to California was a water route that followed the San Juan River and Lake Nicaragua through Nicaragua.

This time, Walker led an "army" of fifty-eight soldiers; but with the addition of native troops, he helped "rescue" the incumbent president and became a military hero. This later led to his being named president. At one point, Walker was the most popular man in Nicaragua. In fact, he became somewhat of a legend. According to one version, the natives were expecting a Messiah, and, long before he came on the scene, they were told a "pale man with cold, gray eyes" would someday come to lead them.

Had he been content to rule only one Central American

country, Walker might have led a long and happy life. Ambition, however, got the better of him; and he died before a Honduran firing squad at the age of thirty-six.

Some historians believe that if "the gray-eyed man of destiny" had succeeded in setting up a single government for Central America, that entire part of the world might have become part of the United States.

25

King's Mountain Messenger

People in today's world have little appreciation for the ways in which the primitive modes of communication in the early days of our country affected daily life. Historians have shown that wars were fought, or prolonged, because of this problem. Whether by horseback or by foot, the modes employed to move information from one place—and person—to another made for some dramatic moments for our forefathers.

For sheer drama, few happenings of early times can match the sight of seven-foot, two-inch Joseph Greer, a Tennessee backwoodsman, walking boldly into the chambers of the Continental Congress and informing the startled members that the Battle of King's Mountain had been won.

Greer is said to have brushed past astonished doorkeepers and guards, marched into the midst of the assembled Congress, and delivered this message: "I am Joseph Greer and came here to tell you that we had a battle on King's Mountain, killed (Major Patrick) Ferguson and killed and captured all his men."

A shout went up from the normally reserved members of the Continental Congress, and Thomas Jefferson was said to have exulted, "The tide has taken a joyful turn!"

And now a little background:

The year was 1780, and America and Great Britain were in the midst of the Revolutionary War. At the time things were not looking good for the home folks. Benedict Arnold had gone over to the enemy, and General Sir Charles Cornwallis was moving through eastern North Carolina with little resistance.

Cornwallis ordered Major Ferguson, who had organized and armed four thousand South Carolina Loyalists, to move into the Watauga country of what now is Tennessee, but at that time was western North Carolina. Then Major Ferguson did a foolish thing. He sent word to the Watauga frontiersmen that he was going to lay waste their settlements and hang their leaders from the nearest tree.

To the likes of John Sevier, colonel of the militia, and Colonel Isaac Shelby, those were indeed fighting words. A call for volunteers was broadcast over the countryside, and a meeting was set for September 25, 1780, at Sycamore Shoals on the Watauga River. When the appointed day arrived, every able-bodied man in the district was there.

Sevier and Shelby, aware of the need for protection on the home front, arranged the first military draft in history. Actually, it was a draft in reverse, in which men were conscripted to stay home. The two colonels kept 240 volunteers each, but they were joined by Virginia troops under Colonel William Campbell and other North Carolinians under Colonel Charles McDowell.

Major Ferguson and his troops took a stand on top of King's Mountain and sent word that he defied "God Almighty and all the rebels out of hell" to overcome him. The frontiersmen charged up the steep mountainside. They had no bayonets, but were skilled in the use of their small bore rifles, tomahawks, and scalping knives. Sevier gave the order to "Shout like hell and fight like devils." According to one account, "the British Army repulsed the waves of determined men again and again, but like hordes of ants, the mountain men charged repeatedly, first from one side of the mountain, then to the other, keeping the British racing back and forth over the craggy peak."

The end came after Ferguson, ignoring pleas of some of his

men to surrender, charged into a group of the mountain men and was cut down by at least six bullets. Chaos set in among his troops and they quickly raised the white flag of surrender.

Samuel Eliot Morrison, author of *The Oxford History of the American People*, writes: "King's Mountain was the Trenton of the Southern campaign, giving new life to an apparently lost cause. Since Cornwallis' advanced position at Charlotte (North Carolina) was now untenable, he hurriedly retreated to Winnsboro, South Carolina."

Theodore Roosevelt, in his book *The Winning of the West*, called it "one of the most important battles that was ever fought on American soil."

Pat Alderman, author of *One Heroic Hour at King's Mountain*, called it "The battle that changed the course of American history." He elaborated: "The fate of American independence hung in the balance during this fateful hour. This victory changed the course of the war. It greatly subdued the Tories of the two Carolinas. News of the battle fired the Americans with fresh zeal and encouraged the fragments of the scattered Army to reorganize and rise anew."

One minor detail remained: getting word of the victory to the Continental Congress. For this assignment, a young twenty-year-old who had participated in the battle, the tall but well-proportioned Joseph Greer, was chosen by John Sevier.

Armed with sword and musket and bearing a brass compass to guide him, Greer set out on his 750-mile journey through uncharted wilderness. Historians disagree on his mode of travel. Some say he started on horseback but had not gone far before Indians shot his horse from under him, forcing him to walk the rest of the way. Others say he walked the entire distance.

Certainly he walked—and ran—most of the way, wading and swimming icy streams and one time evading a group of savage warriors by hiding in a hollow log over which his pursuers ran. In any event, he accomplished his mission.

Opinions differ on Greer's height. His father Andrew, incidentally, was well below average height and was called "wee Andy." William C. Edmiston, author of *Fat of the Land*, says Greer was seven and one-half feet tall. His great-granddaughter, Miss Margaret Boyles, of Nashville, said he was seven feet, two inches.

There's no question he would have made someone a good basketball—or football—player. A display at the Tennessee Museum shows Greer's sword, gun, compass, and a coat. The coat leaves no doubt but that he was indeed a tall man.

After the war, Greer was granted 2,600 acres of land for his services. He traveled into Middle Tennessee and staked his claim in what is now Lincoln County. He built his first home in 1804 and a larger one in 1810—to accommodate himself and his wife and eleven children. The carpenter who built the house received a farm for his work.

A historical marker near Petersburg in Lincoln County has this inscription: "King's Mountain Messenger—About four miles northeast is buried Joseph Greer, son of Andrew Greer, an early member of the Watauga Settlement in East Tennessee. After fighting at King's Mountain, he made a rapid overland trip to Philadelphia, where he officially reported the American victory to the Continental Congress."

26

The War of Faulty Communications

Poor communications played a major role in the War of 1812, from beginning to end. Some even have called it the War of Faulty Communications.

When President James Madison asked Congress on June 1, 1812, to declare war against Great Britain, he listed a number of reasons—Britain's custom of stopping American ships at sea in search of deserting Britons, claims that the British had stirred up Indian warfare in the Northwest, and charges that Britain was interfering with United States trade. Interference with trade was clearly the main reason, and here's where poor communications contributed to the war. Two days before the declaration of war, the British Foreign Minister announced that the Orders in Council—against neutral trade—would be repealed. But the word of that announcement did not reach the United States until after war had been declared.

A good case could also be made for calling it "The Unnecessary War." New England, the part of this country most affected by trade, opposed the war; and this was reflected in the vote by Congress, where those favoring war won by only seventy-nine to forty-nine in the House and nineteen to thirteen in the Senate.

The chorus for war was led by a group of mostly young men from the southern and western states who were known as the "War Hawks." They included such persons as Henry Clay of Kentucky, John C. Calhoun of South Carolina, and Felix Grundy and the elderly John Sevier of Tennessee.

Supporting the War Hawks position was the increasing resistance settlers were meeting from Indians in the Northwest. The evidence strongly indicated that the British were supporting the Indians.

Slow communications also played a major part in the largest engagement of the War of 1812, the Battle of New Orleans. That battle was fought on January 8, 1815, exactly fifteen days after the warring nations had signed a treaty of peace in Ghent, Belgium. This fact has prompted some historians to refer to the Battle of New Orleans as a "needless battle."

Others have argued with equal—or more—vigor that the battle, led by Tennessee's own Andrew Jackson, was both necessary and vital, for the following reasons.

First, a resumé of the battle itself. On the morning of January 8, at six A.M. British General Sir Edward Pakenham led fifty-three hundred troops in a frontal assault on Jackson and his thirty-five hundred men who were dug in on the north bank of the Mississippi River. Jackson and his sharpshooters literally "mowed 'em down," with the result that General Pakenham was killed and two thousand of his men were killed, wounded, or missing. Only thirteen Americans were killed and fifty-eight wounded before the attacking columns melted.

And now, the argument over whether this battle was necessary. Back in the 1930s, a Northerner come south was said to have asked a Nashvillian if it were true that Southerners were still fighting the Civil War—to which the Nashvillian replied, "Heck, we're still fighting the Battle of New Orleans."

What prompted the Nashvillian's remark was that in 1927 the Tennessee General Assembly adopted a resolution authorizing appointment by the governor of a commission composed of persons "of known historical knowledge and research" to make a careful study concerning "the true value of the Battle of New Orleans, fought January 8, 1815."

Named chairman of the study commission was the late Reau Folk who, due to partial retirement, was able to conduct extensive research and prepare a detailed report. The Ladies' Hermitage Association, Nashville, Tennessee, later published the report as *Exposure of Untruth Being Taught Young America*. The report, presented to the Legislature in 1935, quoted a number of historical sources of the day to illustrate the so-called "mis-information" that was being taught schoolchildren and others.

Here were some of the points made in the report as to why the Battle of New Orleans was necessary:

*The Treaty of Ghent stated "in plain language" that "peace shall be effective when the treaty shall have been ratified by both sides." It was ratified by the United States February 17, 1815, forty days after the Battle of New Orleans!"

*In one section of the report titled "Testimony from Andrew Jackson himself," the report quoted from a history of Andrew Jackson by A. C. Buell published in 1904. In this testimony, Jackson told why the battle was essential. Buell quoted Governor William Allen of Ohio on his conversation with Jackson. In this conversation Jackson stated that if British General Pakenham had taken New Orleans, he would have claimed the entire Louisiana Purchase for England. Jackson was quoted further as saying he had learned from diplomatic sources "of the most unquestionable authority" that the British ministry "did not intend for the Treaty of Ghent to apply to the Louisiana Purchase at all."

Buell also quoted from an address by Captain Henry Garland, one of Jackson's officers who had been born and reared in France. Unlike most of the backwoodsmen in Jackson's Army, Captain Garland possessed a good education. In a victory address delivered in French the latter part of March, 1815, in New Orleans, Garland said that before General Pakenham took on Jackson's men, he had a proclamation written and made ready to be delivered in which Britain would claim all of Louisiana.

Folk concluded, on the basis of information "mainly provided by the British themselves," that England held as invalid the title of the United States to Louisiana, acquired by the sale by Napoleon Bonaparte in 1803. Moreover, he said, England deliberately planned the conquest of Louisiana. If successful, England would have developed a great dominion to the west of the United States like Canada on the north.

Another member of the commission, John Trotwood Moore, State Historian, condensed his conclusion into a single sentence: "The Battle of New Orleans saved the Louisiana Purchase, or another war with England."

Judge John H. DeWitt of Nashville, Judge of the Tennessee Court of Appeals, President of the Tennessee Historical Society, and a member of the study commission, wrote Folk: "I fully concur with you in the conclusions stated in your report, as well as the reasons therefor which you have therein set forth in lucid statement."

And now, fifty years after the Folk report was issued, what evidence do we have that it has influenced historians? Very little.

One of the most respected of the history books being taught in Tennessee's high schools, *The American Pageant* by Dr. Thomas Bailey, states, "The slaughter was useless."

And another, *History of a Free People* by Henry W. Bragdon, states. "The Battle of New Orleans, greatest American victory of the War of 1812, was a useless slaughter, for it occurred two weeks after peace had been signed."

Other historians have written along a similar vein: Samuel Eliot Morrison in *The Oxford History of the American People*, says: "This Battle of New Orleans had no military value since peace had already been signed at Ghent on Christmas Eve; but it made a future President of the United States (Jackson) and in folklore wiped out all previous American defeats, ending the 'Second War of Independence.'"

The *World Book Encyclopedia* has a brief section in which it refers to the Battle of New Orleans as "The Needless Battle." *Encyclopedia Britannica* carefully sidesteps the issue, however, saying, "News of the victory reached Washington, D.C., at the same time as that of the Treaty of Ghent and did much to raise the low morale of the capital. The Battle of New Orleans greatly enhanced the reputation of Jackson as a national hero."

So, what can we conclude from all this? It seems that since General Pakenham did not know a truce had been signed and attacked General Jackson and his men, there was no alternative but to resist. Thus the battle was necessary.

We can only speculate as to whether Pakenham would have attacked if he had known of the peace proceedings initiated in Ghent. In any event, poor communications allowed the War of 1812 to begin, and they led to its last—and greatest—battle.

27

A Naval Battle in Tennessee

Contrary to what many Yankees think, the average Southerner will admit that we lost "the War"—finally. But there were some glorious victories for our side, and none more so than the time Nathan Bedford Forrest won a major engagement with the United States Navy.

When people hear that statement, they look incredulously at you, thinking, "You must be off your rocker—Forrest was a cavalryman. How would he be tangling with the Navy anyway?"

The facts are, nevertheless, that there was an encounter and Forrest won a major victory—even by the admission of the Federals.

Here's what happened.

General Forrest employed small artillery seized from the Federals as his principal weapons. He set up operations at Paris Landing on the Tennessee River, using Yankee Parrott guns—cast iron muzzle loaders that threw ten pound shots with considerable accuracy. Forrest set up two groups of Parrott guns on the west bank of the river, leaving a stretch of open river between them.

When a steamer came into the trap with two barges of supplies, Forrest's men fired from both ends of the trap until the boat was beached on the east bank. Everyone fled except the captain. One of Forrest's men tied a pistol around his neck and paddled over on a slab of wood. He brought the captain back aboard a captured yawl that was also used to tow the ship to the west bank.

The same trap caught a transport and its convoying gunboat and held them while troops fired small arms from the banks in a six-hour battle. With the captured supplies, Forrest moved his guns up to Johnsonville with some of his men going by river in captured boats. The guns were set up on the west bank in carefully chosen locations. A Confederate shot exploded the boiler of a gunboat. Two other gunboats were set afire and drifted against transports, setting these ablaze. Another gunboat ran to the landing, and her crew kept on running. Two steamers were set afire by other shots. The Federals finally set fire to their last boat.

Four gunboats, eight or more transports, and twelve barges were lost by the Federals, along with a fort manned by a 700-man garrison and an unknown number of casualties. The Confederates lost only two killed and nine wounded. Forrest estimated damage to the Federals of $6,000,000, and they admitted a loss of $2,000,000. More importantly, a supply route badly needed for the Nashville-Chattanooga-Atlanta route to the sea was out of commission for the remainder of the war.

The engagement took place on November 4, 1864. The *Tennessee Blue Book* carries an item stating simply, "Forrest's Cavalry Defeats Federal Navy at Johnsonville."

According to reliable reports, some of the hulls are still embedded in the bottom of the river, now better known as Kentucky Lake.

PART SIX:

Law and Disorders

Outlaw John Murrell in
the act of stealing a slave
and, with a confederate,
disposing of the body of a
robbery victim.

28

The "Genteel" Outlaw

Of all the outlaws of the early years of Tennessee and the Natchez Trace, there was none to compare with John A. Murrell, a man of such "genteel manners" he could pass as a minister of the gospel. Yet his cunning and evil brain was forever cooking up some new plot that often led to robbery and murder.

John Murrell was a "native son" of Tennessee, born near Columbia and on or near the Natchez Trace. His life of crime began at an early age. His mother, who ran a hotel of sorts, was something of a "Fagin," teaching little John and her other children to rob from the guests. John became so adept at picking locks that he could rummage through a sleeping guest's belongings without arousing him.

His mother's teachings boomeranged against her, however. When Murrell reached the age of sixteen, he robbed the family treasury of fifty dollars and headed for Nashville. By an odd coincidence, one of his victims recognized him as he walked along the Public Square; but he was apparently impressed at the boy's skill and invited him to join him in a horse-thieving operation along the Wilderness Road.

Along the way, the thieves fell in with a talkative young trader from South Carolina who made the mistake of telling them he had been to Tennessee to purchase some hogs but had decided against buying any and was returning with his money. At an opportune moment, the two set upon the hapless South Carolinian, stunning him with a lead-weighted whip and then tossing his body down a ravine, after first relieving him of some $1,262.

Murrell later recalled that they did not have time to kill the man. However, he became more careful in later years, always killing his victim to prevent possible future testimony against him and disposing of the body by filling it with rocks and tossing it into a nearby river.

Murrell was most noted for his dealings as a slave thief. By his own estimate, he stole more than one hundred. Over the years, he built an "organization" of more than one hundred persons from Nashville to Arkansas and south through Mississippi and Louisiana to New Orleans.

With the help of his organization, he almost pulled off a massive slave uprising in which, at a specified time, slaves were to turn on their owners and massacre them. The motive had nothing to do with freedom of the slaves, but rather the creation of pandemonium in which looting would be easier to accomplish. Word of the diabolical plot leaked out, however, and it was never put into action.

Murrell's unsavory practices made it possible for him to ride the finest horses, wear expensive clothing, and make frequent visits to Memphis, Natchez, and New Orleans.

One stratagem he learned from a New Orleans friend was to dress as a preacher, conduct revivals, and trade his "soul-saving" services for hard cash. He also found that by posing as a man of the cloth, he could win respect from strangers more quickly for ordinary business dealings. Many of his deals involved the passing of counterfeit bills to his trusting victims.

Like another infamous outlaw, Jesse James, Murrell fell the victim of a confidant. On June 1, 1833, a young man by the name of Virgil Stewart set out from Jackson, Tennessee, on horseback with the objective of catching up with Murrell on a journey to the west. He was to make friends with him and turn him over to the law. Stewart accomplished his mission in a daring trip to one of Murrell's secret hideaways in Arkansas.

Murrell was brought to trial, convicted of slave-stealing and selling, and sentenced to ten years in the State Penitentiary in Nashville.

29
The Wyoming Wild Bunch

While Butch Cassidy and his Wyoming Wild Bunch pulled most of their antics in the West, Tennessee was an involuntary host to at least two and perhaps more of the desperadoes.

Kid Curry, whose real name was Harvey Logan, and who was Cassidy's right hand man (ranking above the Sundance Kid), entered Tennessee in his flight from the law, winding up in Knoxville.

While Kid Curry entertained himself in a solitary game of pool, a skill at which he was apparently not as proficient as with his deadly six-gun, two onlookers began to snicker at his playing. Curry attacked them with a cue stick. Two policemen moved in, and he shot them both, escaping out a rear door. In the process, he slid down an embankment and wrenched his ankle.

It was in the dead of winter in the year 1901, and a posse overtook Kid Curry near Jefferson City. They succeeded in placing the West's deadliest gunman behind bars in Knoxville for the only time in his life in any jail. At the request of the government, the Pinkerton Detective Agency sent one of its men, Lowell Spence, to identify the Kid.

As Spence entered the cellblock, Curry stared at him and said, "Hello, Spence." Spence said, "Hello, Kid," to which Curry replied, "When I get out, I'll be waiting for you."

Coming from a gunman who had once traveled two hundred miles to carry out a similar promise to gun down someone who had fingered him, this was no idle threat. And Spence knew it.

A few days later, the Kid got his chance to escape when a guard ventured too near his cell. Curry took a coil of wire he had taken from a broom and lassoed the guard. He took the key to his cell and two six-shooters and was soon on his way back to the wild, wild West.

Before he could make good on his threat to kill Spence, Curry became embroiled in a gun battle and was shot. While lying wounded on a grassy meadow, he was heard to yell to his friends, "Don't wait for me." He then killed himself.

Later, a dispute over whether the dead man was Curry led to the Adams Express Company's insisting that Pinkerton exhume the body to check the teeth for identification. This was done, and it proved to be Curry indeed.

Meanwhile, another equally unsavory member of the Cassidy gang, largest and most dangerous in the history of the West, also visited Tennessee. Deaf Charley Hanks, who once killed a man for laughing at his disability, was in Memphis briefly in 1901. He then moved on to Nashville, where he was almost captured while trying to cash a stolen government bond in a Nashville bank. He escaped after a mad race through downtown Nashville in a stolen icewagon, after which he commandeered a boat to cross the Cumberland River.

Another pair of the Cassidy gang, Ben Kilpatrick, "the tall Texan," and his common-law wife, Laura Bullion, once gave their home address as Memphis, although there is no proof they ever lived there.

The Tennessee visits came after the Wild Bunch had been broken up following an all-out campaign in the "Hole-in-the-Wall" area of Wyoming directed by the governors of Wyoming, Colorado, and Utah.

And what about Butch Cassidy and the Sundance Kid (Harry Longbaugh)? They went South of the Border for a continued life of robbing trains and banks and rustling cattle. The end came in an encounter with a detachment of the Bolivian cavalry. The Kid was mortally wounded, and Cassidy took his own life with his .45 revolver after being hopelessly surrounded by the soldiers.

They were buried side by side in the San Vicente Cemetery, a single headboard at their graves bearing the two names, "Cassidy" and "Longbaugh." Under each name was added "Bandido Yanqui."

30

Jesse James Helps a Widow Outsmart "Scrooge"

Once described by a Kansas City newspaper as "the world's most famed bandit," Jesse James became such a living legend that it is difficult to tell how many of the stories told about him were true and how many were just plain fiction. But there is some indication that an incident in which he was said to have helped a poor Tennessee widow pay off the mortgage on her farm really happened.

It is chronicled not only in the book, *The Rise and Fall of Jesse James,* by Robertus Love, but also in a book written by Jesse James, Jr., entitled *Jesse James, My Father—the First and Only True Story of His Adventures.* It was probably this incident that caused the songwriter to say that James "robbed from the rich and gave to the poor." The way in which it happened, however, might lead one to suspect that the Missouri outlaw did it to satisfy his love of a practical joke.

According to the story, James and a companion were traveling through "the mountain districts of Tennessee" and stopped for lunch at a farm owned by the widow of one of James' fellow guerrillas under William C. Quantrill, the leader of a band of Confederates who operated independently during the Civil War.

The lady seemed very despondent and, under questioning by Jesse James, said her problem was that she owed five hundred dollars that was due that very day. The sheriff and the money lender were on the way to foreclose the mortgage. James very gallantly reached into his pocket and produced the necessary five hundred dollars, insisting that she accept his generosity and not give it another thought.

Before departing, he obtained a good description of the sheriff and "Scrooge" and the route they would be taking to the farm.

James and his companion picked a secluded spot beside the road leading to the widow's farm, watched the two men go by in their buggy and then begin the return journey. As they came even with the bandits, the two men jumped out of the bushes, pulled their six-guns on them, and relieved them of the five hundred dollars, ordering them to proceed back to town.

Most people have heard the story of how "the dirty little coward," Robert Ford, shot James in the back as he dusted a picture, but he had many close calls during his charmed existence.

One of the most hair-raising occurred on a hot summer afternoon when James and a companion yielded to the temptation to shed their clothing and take a dip in a river that ran alongside the road they were traveling. As they enjoyed the cooling waters of the river and chatted, they were suddenly brought back to reality with a stern order from the bank to "throw up your hands."

James, with ten thousand dollars on his head, found himself looking at the business end of a double-barreled shotgun wielded by a person who seemed to have every intention of collecting.

But the two bandits had been in tight places before and seemed to have a way of communicating with each other without benefit of the spoken word. James started wading ashore, his hands up and maintaining a steady flow of conversation in which he tried to convince his adversary that all this was entirely unnecessary. As his companion remained in the water with arms raised, James approached the gunman, maintaining his dignity despite his state of dishabille

This photo of Jesse James, taken in Nebraska City, Nebraska, in 1875, was the last known photo taken of the outlaw.

and seeming indignant over the fact that two gentlemen couldn't enjoy a quiet bath after a hard day of riding.

As if it had all been planned, James' companion suddenly gave a shrill whoop and dived under the water. The gunman momentarily turned to determine the cause of the commotion, and James leaped upon him.

As the two men grappled—one fully clothed and the other in the altogether—James'companion rushed to his aid; and soon the tables were completely turned. They disarmed the man, gave him a ducking in the water, put on their clothing—and weapons—and went on their way.

Many of the stories told about Jesse James were completely false. People were particularly prone to visualize him as the leader of every train robbery that took place from Chicago to California. On the day he was killed, for instance, there was a news item out of Texas in which a victim of a train holdup identified his assailant as Jesse James, an event that could only have taken place with the benefit of a jet plane in that year of 1882.

So intense was the feeling about the colorful desperado that years after his death his son, Jesse, Jr., a clean-living, law-abiding young fellow who had spent the better part of his life earning respectability, was accused and tried in a court of law on a trumped-up charge of taking part in a train robbery.

31

Big Walton and the Law

Constable Churchwell moved through the crowded courtroom with a sheepish look on his face. Behind his desk, his red hair ablaze with reflected sunlight from the glassless window behind his seat, sat the judge. He idly toyed with the heavy wooden mallet he was using as a gavel and fixed an unblinking stare on Churchwell.

"Well, Constable," he snapped, "are you ready with your next case?"

"Yer honor," Churchwell began, in a high-pitched whine, "I have some bad news to report. The prisoner escaped last night, so I guess we can't have his trial today, after all."

"Escaped," the judge thundered, and his eyes took on a gleam that made the constable hang his head. "What steps have you taken to recapture him?"

"Well," said the constable. "You see, Big Walton not only escaped, he took four pair of pistols out of the jail with him. We know where he is. He is sitting under a tree up on Walnut Hill right now, but he's already shot at me and a deputy, and he says he'll kill any man that comes up there."

"By the Almighty," shouted the judge, his face turning almost the color of his hair. "Do you mean to stand there and tell me you can't arrest this man?"

"Well, your honor, we ain't been able to yet . . ."

"Constable," the judge roared. "You are the law here. You

can deputize any man you want . . . and as many as you need to get the job done! Don't you know you can even deputize a judge off his bench to make an arrest if you can't carry out the law by yourself?"

The constable shuffled his feet, then, looking the judge straight in the eye, said, "All right, sir, I deputize you, then, to go out and arrest Big Walton and bring him in to trial."

"Very well, then," shouted the judge. "Court's recessed for one hour." Leaping to his feet, he quickly shed his black robe and stamped through the crowded courtroom to the door.

Minutes later, Big Walton looked up from his seat beneath the tree on Walnut Hill. He glanced at the guns laid out before him and the jug of whiskey near his right hand.

Looking down the hill, he saw a strange procession heading his way. In front was the red-haired judge, his arms swinging widely. Some twenty feet behind him the constable followed, and still some distance behind him came a crowd of townspeople, keeping well in the background but close enough to observe what was happening. Big Walton took a slug from his jug and then picked up one of his weapons.

"Walton," said the judge in an authoritative tone of voice. "Put down that gun. I've come to arrest you."

Before he could raise the pistol, the judge reached forward and grabbed him by the shirt front. With a quick jerk, he brought the big man to his feet. The gun fell to the ground.

"All right, all right," Walton mumbled, drunkenly. "I'll come along."

And he allowed the constable to take the other arm as they led him off to trial in Township Court, Greeneville, Tennessee, Judge Andrew Jackson presiding.

32
Early Tennessee Punishments

Had some of our present-day moralists lived in Tennessee during the early 1800s, they might have admonished grownups to tie their reins securely to the hitching rails and thus avoid tempting a youth to go wrong. For then, as now, there were young bucks around—and some older ones—who would make off with another's mode of transport if the opportunity presented itself.

But, unlike today's car thief who may get a light sentence for a first offense, the horse thief was severely punished, even when the animal was taken briefly for a "joyride" or used to finish plowing a field. The common treatment was to give the offender a public lashing at the whipping post, nail his ears to a board, and brand his right cheek with the letter *H*, his left with the letter, *T*.

This treatment was primarily for first offenders. The "pros" who made a practice of stealing horses and selling them for a profit were often hanged. Murderers usually got off with less severe punishment. If two men became involved in a brawl and if one of them, perchance, should clout the other with a pole or other weapon resulting in his death, he would normally get off with a public lashing or be branded on the left hand or cheek with the letter *M* for murderer. The pesky brands were hard to live with. About the only remedy was to grow a beard and cover them.

The reason for the heavy punishment of horse thieves is not difficult to see in view of the extent to which the early settlers depended on their animals. Horse power was the only kind—for pulling a plow to eke out a livelihood, for hauling produce and goods to and from the cities and towns, for pulling a carriage, or for riding. The old phrase, "My kingdom for a horse" might better have been changed to say "My horse is half my kingdom."

Another form of punishment was the pillory, a frame of adjustable boards with openings large enough to insert the offender's head and hands. Both Nashville and Knoxville had pillories and public whipping posts, and there were probably others.

One advantage of these devices over jails (or gaols as they were spelled then after the common custom in the old country) was that a man could get his punishment over in a short time and be returned to the labor force, which was severely limited.

In a typical public whipping, the hands of the guilty person were fastened to the ends of a horizontal piece of a cross. His back was bared, and the number of lashes prescribed by the court were "well laid on" by the sheriff. The poor sheriff also had the chore of conducting all public hangings.

Any kind of stealing was looked upon as a serious offense. A man received thirty-nine lashes for stealing a handkerchief, and a woman nine lashes for stealing six pounds of "soape" worth two pence (four cents) and three ounces of "sewing thread."

33

A Test of Tennessee Dog Laws

The setting was a mountain top in Grundy County. The year was 1848. If you're not familiar with that part of the state, it may help to know that Grundy is the home county of Monteagle and Tracy City, and some of its forests have changed little since the event we're about to relate.

Early on a Monday morning in the month of April, Judge Sam Anderson arrived at the crude building which served as the courthouse for Grundy County. He noted with satisfaction that the docket contained only one case. No doubt he could wind up his business in short order and be on his way back to his home court sixty miles away.

"Are the parties present?" the judge inquired of the sheriff, who replied that plaintiff and defendant were, indeed, present, along with eight lawyers, forty witnesses, and the dog Sharp.

This latter reference caused the judge to lift an eyebrow. After the jury had been excused to a nearby woods for lack of better accommodations, he inquired what the case was about.

Judge Anderson was informed that the case was an appeal from a verdict by a justice of the peace in which he ruled that the owner of Sharp, a yellow mongrel, was entitled to ten dollars in damages for injuries inflicted by the defendant's hounds.

It seems that Sharp had been returning from a hunt when the hounds attacked him, causing him to partially lose his hearing. Since Sharp was a "slow track" dog and of great value to his master, who derived his livelihood from hunting, this was a most serious loss, at least according to his attorneys.

After much arguing between the lawyers, Sharp's character was put in issue. Thereupon, a procession of witnesses came forward to tell how the canine had been observed robbing tanyards and breaking into springhouses (no refrigerators or even iceboxes, yet). Some had even seen him in the neighborhood where sheep had been killed by a marauder.

Witnesses for the plaintiff told what a fine, loyal dog Sharp was, and the attorneys waxed eloquent describing the joy he brought his master, his wife, and children upon returning from a hunt—back before his faculties were impaired by the defendant's impetuous hounds.

Testimony dragged on for three days and the arguments continued into Saturday before the case was concluded.

Judge Anderson's charge to the jury was an eloquent, though carefully phrased, one. While references had been made by both sides to the "Tennessee Dog Law," he was not sure, despite forty years of legal practice and sitting on the bench, what the alleged law stated.

A chief contention by counsel for the plaintiff was that any dog found guilty of killing sheep was *per se* infamous and fair game for anyone possessing a weapon that would slay him.

But Judge Anderson pointed out that they were hampered, due to the remoteness of their location, by the absence of any authoritative source for checking the law. Meanwhile, he ruled that the jury should give weight to the matter of whether Sharp may have been making his raids on springhouses or attacking sheep to assuage his hunger, or if it were done through malice aforethought. The judge released the jury to its deliberations with the reminder that the case had already gone into its sixth day and a verdict with all deliberate speed would be welcomed.

Despite the fact that they retired this time to the town's saloon, the jury very quickly came back with a verdict—$2.50 for the plaintiff.

But the real jolt was to come the next morning after the clerk wrote up the minutes—$320 in court costs to be shared by both parties.

When you consider how many current dollars it would take to be the equivalent of those $320 in 1848, it is not hard to believe the sad end to the story. Both men went bankrupt, and five years later they were still filing claims and counterclaims!

34

Those Terrible Harpes and Their Women

Our TV-tutored generation seems to think all the bad guys used to be in the West and that the first gangs operated out of Chicago. We aren't particularly proud of it; but, for the record, Tennessee had its share of the world's meanest outlaws. It would be difficult to say which among them qualified for the title, "Worst All-round Guys."

A good candidate for the title would be the Harpe brothers—Micajah, better known as "Big Harpe," and Wiley, known to all during that hectic period of Tennessee's early statehood as "Little Harpe." The antics of these fellows and their traveling female companions make Bonnie and Clyde sound like the Bobbsey Twins. The terror occasioned by "Those terrible men, the Harpes" was so widespread that a large area of Tennessee and Kentucky literally rose up in arms, killing scores of suspects, many of them innocent, before the real objects of the chase were captured.

It was about 1795, a year before Tennessee became a state, that the Harpes and their two girl friends, Susan and Betsy Roberts, left their North Carolina home to come to Tennessee. The four took up with a renegade tribe of Cherokee Indians, living dangerously for two years, dodging the bullets of white settlers and the arrows of the organized Indian tribes.

After leaving their Indian hosts, the Harpe brothers and their women chose a lonely section of the Wilderness Road leading into Knoxville to begin their life of crime. Their first victim was a young Methodist circuit rider, and the robbery differed from subsequent ones in that they merely took his money and his horse and neglected to murder him. Future victims were not so fortunate. The Harpes adopted the strategy, later followed by John Murrell and others, of killing their victims as a matter of course so there would be no witnesses to testify against them. Often they employed a trick learned from their Indian friends of tomahawking the hapless wayfarers whom they robbed. Their method of disposing of the bodies was also usually effective—cutting them open, filling the bodies with sand or gravel, and tossing them into the river.

Although the Harpes were presumably married to the Roberts sisters, Little Harpe became enamored of a third girl, a young blond daughter of a minister. After a summer of courtship, he was married to her, with the preacher-father performing the ceremony. The presence of the extra girl seemed to create no triangle problems, and the little band of marauders became a party of five.

After murder number five, a posse went after the Harpes. The men and their wives—all three pregnant—offered no resistance and were jailed in Danville, Kentucky. A couple of months later, the men escaped, leaving the jailer to care for their three wives and three bouncing babies.

When the women came to trial, the townspeople took pity on them and they were acquitted. The three women and their babies disappeared in a canoe, and before long they had taken up with their menfolk again.

There were more robbery-murders and rewards of three hundred dollars each (a lot of money in those days) were posted for the two men. Posses were formed in many counties of Kentucky and Tennessee.

One of the strangest tales of all concerned a confrontation between the Harpe group—there were eight of them now, counting the babes in arms—and a posse. When the two groups suddenly met in a dense wooded area, the men in the posse suddenly lost their nerve and walked past them without lifting a hand.

Another posse had better leadership. Moses Steigal, who lived in the area near Eddyville, Kentucky, had once been a confederate of the Harpes. They repaid him by killing his wife and child and burning down his house. After posseman Samuel Leiper fired the shot that felled Big Harpe, Steigal beheaded Harpe with Harpe's own butcher knife. He slung the head into a bag, put it across his saddle, and took it into a settlement that later was named, quite appropriately, Harpeshead.

Little Harpe, meanwhile, made his escape. But he was later tracked down along the Natchez Trace, hanged, and beheaded.

The women, an obviously hardy lot, lived to ripe old ages. Presumably two of the children did, too. Big Harpe confessed during his dying moments that he killed one of them because it wouldn't stop crying.

35
Moonshine Tales

Back in the heyday of moonshine whiskey, Tennessee had its share of those who distilled and sold the spirits as both an avocation and a vocation. One of Tennessee's counties, Cocke, was once known as the moonshine capital of the world.

We've all heard of the "revenooers" who searched out the stills and the people who operated them, the "shiners." The problem stemmed from the federal laws that require those who manufacture and distill spirits to register their "plants," however small, and pay a tax on their product.

At one time a good many of the "shiners" complied with the law. Their operations were profitable, and they could afford to pay a tax as part of the cost of doing business. Unfortunately, the price of sugar, a primary ingredient—along with corn—of the mash, kept rising as did the tax on liquor; so many of the "producers" found that the most practical way to stay in business was to avoid the tax. As a result, the federal courts of the state became deluged with criminal cases of those charged by grand juries with violating the federal internal revenue laws relating to intoxicating liquors.

Those brought into court were charged with such violations as manufacturing whiskey in an unregistered distillery, carrying on the business of a distiller without having posted the required bond, working in an unregistered distillery, and possessing whiskey on which the tax had not been paid. Some of the charges were felonies carrying severe penalties.

Aware of the severe penalties prescribed for conviction, suspected moonshiners created some highly imaginative stories to explain why they happened to be in the vicinity of a still at the time the revenue agents made a raid.

Here are just a few of them:

* "I was just out hunting ginseng and happened upon this here still. I didn't have nothing to do with it."

* "I came up on this here still and was gittin' me a drink of the beer when the revenooers raided it" (beer is the residue left by the fermenting mash).

* (If the agents saw the suspect stirring the cooking mash in the still, catching him red-handed as it were): "I just happened by and saw the still. I never saw one before and wanted to look in the pot to see what it looked like while it cooked."

* (Many of the apparatuses used an old car radiator as a crucial part of the process, leading to the following alibi): "My ole car's got a busted radiator, and I thought maybe I could take this one if nobody came up for a while."

* (While being caught tinkering with a still or operating one is damning evidence, it is within the law to express an intention to operate one, hence this explanation): "I was planning to set up a still and was getting me a 'worm' for one" (A "worm" is the copper tubing for a still).

While we tend to think of moonshiners as a motley, shiftless lot, not all of them were. Some, in fact, were "upstanding citizens" in their communities, active in their churches and in public affairs. They were considered men of integrity whose word was their bond. And some did, indeed, consider themselves law-abiding citizens in every sense of the word.

This brings us to still another "excuse" that fair-minded judges had difficulty rejecting. These suspects were certain that they had a right to make moonshine because their ancestors did it: "Pa did it, and his Pa before him done it. I've been told by the family that all of 'em did it 'way back to the time of the War, and none of them ever got arrested for it or had to go off to jail."

That opinion, passed down through several generations, stemmed from a commonly held belief that as a pension for service in the Revolutionary War, veterans were issued exemption certificates giving them the right to make whiskey. It was assumed that these certificates exempted them from having to register their stills, make bond, or pay any federal tax.

The mountain folk also believed this exemption constituted "property" of their ancestors. As such it could be inherited by the descendants of the exempted veteran. Since many Revolutionary soldiers were given large tracts of land that grew immensely in value as generations came and went, this claim by the moonshiners was modest and reasonable, indeed. And these otherwise upstanding citizens greatly resented the fact that they were regarded as criminals for "doing what they always done."

Bibliography

Aiken, Leona, *Donelson, Tennessee, Its History and Landmarks*. Nashville: Donelson History Books Committee, 1968.

Alderman, Pat, *One Heroic Hour at King's Mountain*. Erwin, Tennessee: Pat Alderman, 1968.

Barr, Thomas C., Jr., *Tennessee Caves*. Nashville: Department of Geology, Tennessee Department of Conservation, 1961, 1972.

Brown, Frank, Jr., *Unto These Hills*. Cherokee, North Carolina: Brochure, Cherokee Historical Association, 1984.

Burton, Thomas G., *The Hanging of Mary, a Circus Elephant*. Johnson City: Tennessee Folklore Society Bulletin, 1971.

Coppock, Paul R., *Memphis Sketches*. Memphis: Friends of the Memphis and Shelby County Public Libraries, 1976.

Creekmore, Betsey Beeler, *Knoxville*. Knoxville: University of Tennessee Press, 1958, 1967.

Creighton, Wilbur F., Creighton, Wilbur F., Jr., and Johnson, Leland R., *Building of Nashville*. Nashville: Wilbur F. Creighton, Jr., 1969.

Faulkner, Charles H., *The Old Stone Fort*. Knoxville: University of Tennessee Press, 1966.

Folk, Reau, "Exposure of Untruth Being Taught Young America." Paper presented to the Tennessee State Legislature, Nashville, 1935.

Guild, Jo Conn, *Old Times in Tennessee*. Nashville: Tavel, Eastman and Howell, 1878.

McMahan, Basil B., *The Mystery of the Old Stone Fort*. Nashville: Tennessee Book Company, 1965.

Morrow, Sara S., *The Legacy of Fannie Battle*. Nashville: Fannie Battle Social Workers, 1980.

Phelan, James, *History of Tennessee*. Boston: Houghton-Mifflin Company, 1889.

Putnam, A.W., *History of Middle Tennessee*. Knoxville: University of Tennessee Press, 1971.

Ramsey, J. F. M., *The Annals of Tennessee to the End of the 18th Century*. Charleston: Walker and James, 1853.

Sloan, John E., *The Sloan Family*. Nashville: The Nashville Room, The Public Library of Nashville and Davidson County, 1980.

Suppiger, Joseph E., *Phoenix of the Mountains, The Story of Lincoln Memorial University*. Harrogate, Tennessee: Lincoln Memorial University Press, 1977.

Warden, Margaret Lindsley, *The Dickinson Family*. Nashville: The Nashville Room, The Public Library of Nashville and Davidson County, 1983.

Waters, Charles M., *Historic Clarksville: The Bicentennial Story, 1784-1984*. Clarksville: Historic Clarksville Publishing Company, 1984.

Wheeler, Mary Bray, "The Literature of the Cherokee Indians." Paper, Atlanta, Georgia, 1959.

Williams, Samuel Cole, *History of the Lost State of Franklin*. New York: The Press of the Pioneers, 1933.

Index

143